SEASONS
OF THE ESKIMO

SEASONS
OF THE ESKIMO

A VANISHING WAY of life

photography and text by fred bruemmer

New York Graphic Society Ltd., Greenwich Connecticut

Standard Book Number 8212-0298-7
Library of Congress
Catalog Card Number 78-162720

For permission to reprint material from Knud Rasmussen's *Fifth
Thule Expedition Report* (Gyldendal, Copenhagen), grateful
acknowledgement is made to the heirs of the author.

PRINTED AND BOUND IN ITALY

To Ekalun
and the other Eskimos of Bathurst Inlet
who shared with me their tents, their food,
and their wisdom of life on the land.

CONTENTS

INTRODUCTION

In the beginning, man was a hunter, "a cunning hunter" as the Bible says of Esau. For all but a tiny fraction of the more than a million years since man emerged as a hunting hominid on the African veld, his existence has been ruled and his character stamped by the iron law that nature has laid down for all predators: to live they must kill. A tundra wolf must kill at least sixteen caribou a year in order to survive. An inland Eskimo had to kill two hundred caribou annually to keep himself, his family, and his dogs alive.

As a predator, man is poorly equipped by nature. He lacks fangs and claws. Most prey animals are faster than he. For success in hunting, early man depended on his ability to think and plan, on the crude weapons he fashioned, wooden clubs and roughly chipped pebbles, and on organized co-operation with the other men in his small hunting group.

Like other predators, man had to live in balance with his prey. If he became too successful and diminished the game, hunting became more precarious and his numbers declined until the balance had been re-established. It was a hard and risky existence, and scientists estimate early man had a lifespan of only about twenty-five years.

Not until he developed agriculture, some ten thousand years ago, was man freed from the constant pressure to hunt for meat. Only then could his numbers increase rapidly. Nature lost her control over him and he bent her laws to his will, though not always to his ultimate advantage. The population of the hunting people of the harsh but game-rich North American Arctic was about one person per 250 square miles before the advent of white man. (In Holland now the population density is more than nine hundred people per square mile.)

In the United States today eight percent of the people produce more than enough food to feed themselves and the other ninety-two percent of the population, to whom food is simply something they acquire by walking to the nearest supermarket. In primitive hunting societies, the need to procure food required the incessant effort of all the men, and even then, in a life dependent upon the vagaries of weather and game, the fear of famine was never far.

If the life of the hunter was hard, with an ample measure of danger and despair, it had its compensations. His was, essentially, an egalitarian society in which a man's worth was judged by his wisdom and his skill as a hunter. Material possessions, apart from a few essential tools and weapons, were a hindrance rather than an asset to a people who had to migrate frequently in order to make maximum use of game available. The ethnologist Diamond Jenness tells of an acquisitive Eskimo on Victoria Island who had amassed so many goods his dogs could barely move the loaded sled. Had he not numbered among his possessions several sturdy wives, admirably suited to hauling, he would not have been able to make the vital migrations.

The farmer's life, sated and sedentary, offers security, drudgery, and boredom. The hunter's life was precarious, but exciting. Only he knew the thrill and tension of the stealthy stalk, the wild, heart-pounding race to run down a wounded animal and the climactic exultation of the kill. Then a man had food again. That pride in himself as a hunter has been vividly expressed in an Eskimo poem:

> A wonderful occupation
> Hunting caribou!
> But all too rarely we
> Excel at it
> So that we stand
> Like a bright flame
> Over the plain.

The size of the early hunting communities depended upon the number and type of game available. It required many men to stampede wild horses over a cliff or to build an elaborate pound to catch and kill bison. Mammoth hunters of eastern Russia lived in villages of one hundred people and more. The Eskimos at Bering Strait hunted walrus and sixty-ton bowhead whales. There, one successful hunt alone could provide substantial feasts for a good-sized settlement.

Where game is scarce, or small in size, hunting groups, too, are small and widely dispersed. A lean spring caribou is but one meal for an Eskimo family and its dogs. The solitary hunter is rare. A single accident could mean his death and that of his family. If hunting fails, he quickly weakens, his trips become shorter, his chances of success smaller; and the more desperately he needs food, the less likely he is to get it. When several hunting families live together, chances that at least one man will be successful are enhanced, and the food is shared by the community.

Since man originated in Africa, he has been basically a warm-weather animal. As he spread into Europe and northern Asia, he encountered cold weather which nature had never equipped him to endure. A naked man exposed to sub-zero temperature and wind will die in a few minutes. But rather than travel the slow evolutionary road of developing a densely furred, cold-resistant human strain, man took the short cut of clothing himself in the warm skins of animals adapted to the cold.

During the last of the Pleistocene's four Ice Ages, mile-thick glaciers covered most of Canada and a portion of the United States. Eight million cubic miles of water were locked within the monstrous ice sheets, and the level of the world's oceans was three hundred feet lower than it is now. North America was a great peninsula of the Eurasian continent, linked to it by a thousand-mile-wide land bridge—the now vanished country of Beringia. Unlike eastern and central North America, most of Alaska, Beringia, and Siberia were free of ice.

Immense herds of animals grazed on these ice-free plains: caribou, bison, muskoxen, and shaggy, dome-headed mammoth. Pursuing them, proto-Mongolian hunters from eastern Siberia crossed into the New World about 28,000 years ago. Over the millennia, these ancestors of today's Indians spread to every region of the vast and empty continent, down to its very tip at Tierra del Fuego. But after three or four thousand years, the door to further immigration from Asia closed. Precipitation increased, the glaciers grew thicker and crept down from the Rocky Mountains to the western sea. A wall of ice barred the route to the north for more than ten thousand years.

As the ice receded, hunters from the south followed the herds of game northward. One day, perhaps in northern British Columbia, or southern Alaska, they met another people, the newest wave of Siberian immigrants, who may have still been able to cross on the land bridge before it disappeared under the rising waters which now as the Bering Strait separate the continents of America and Asia. Possibly these new arrivals were the ancestors of today's Athapaskan Indians.

The Eskimos' forbears, presumed to have been a Mongoloid racial group (their legacy is the bluish Mongolian spot near the base of the spine with which every Eskimo baby is born), arrived in Alaska about eight thousand years ago. The land bridge had probably disappeared by then, but it had left two convenient stepping stones, Big Diomede Island (now Russian) and, two miles away, little Diomede Island (now American), in the fifty-seven-mile-wide Bering Strait, making boat crossings relatively easy. From these early arrivals, whom some scientists call proto-Eskimos, the Eskimos and the Aleuts evolved. They now speak two widely diverging languages, but linguists, using the forbiddingly named lexicostatistical method of glottochronology, claim both evolved from the same language spoken some five to six thousand years ago.

Archeologists, who are also good at coining complicated terms, call the first discernible proto-Eskimo culture the Cape Denbigh Complex of the Arctic Small Tool Tradition. (This culture is occasionally referred to as the Campus culture, since its first artifacts were discovered on the present site of the University of Alaska near Fairbanks.)

From Alaska, the Denbigh people spread eastward along the Arctic coasts leaving, as telltale testimony to their passing, distinctively fashioned, tiny stone tools, such as burins, microblades, and arrowheads, superbly chipped from chert or obsidian. By 2000 B.C., they had reached northeastern Greenland, and their reign over most of the Arctic lasted for another 1,200 years.

From the people of the Arctic Small Tool Tradition emerged a new culture, about 800 B.C., probably in the Foxe Basin area of northern Hudson Bay. It has been called the Dorset culture, since its first recognized artifacts came from Cape Dorset in southern Baffin Island. It spread west nearly as far as the Mackenzie Delta, east to Greenland, and south along the coast of Labrador and across Belle Isle Strait to northern Newfoundland.

The Dorsets were distinctly Eskimoan. They heated their semi-subterranean winter homes with blubber-burning, crescentic soapstone lamps; they may have invented the igloo and they used skin-boats, but they probably had no dogs and pulled their small ivory-shod sleds themselves.

These were the Eskimos that the Vikings met on their voyages to Vinland. When the Norseman Karlsefni camped at Hop,

probably in Newfoundland, nine skin-boats with Skraelings, as the Vikings called the natives, arrived. "They were swarthy people and queer-looking, and the hair of their head was ugly. They had remarkable eyes and broad cheeks," Eirik the Red's saga records.

In Eskimo folklore, the Dorset people live on as a race of giants, the Tunit. They were so powerful, the tales tell, they could haul a harpooned walrus home as if it were a mere seal. The Eskimos of the Igloolik area say that before their ancestors came to the land where they now live, "it was inhabited by a great and strong people called Tunit. They lived in stone houses in winter, and were mighty men in all manner of hunting. But they were very quarrelsome, and easily angered. At first the tribes lived peaceably together down by the coast, but the Tunit were too easily angered, and were at last driven out of the country."

Surprisingly, these irascible giants were superb artists, perhaps the best the Arctic has ever seen, who carved with simple stone tools exquisite miniature figurines in ivory, bone, or wood, of falcons, and bears, and men, some less than an inch in size.

For the incredible span of nearly two thousand years, people of the Dorset culture were masters of most of the Arctic. About 900 A.D. competition arrived from the west, smaller men perhaps (the sagas describe them as dwarfish), but courageous and inventive. Beginning their invasion from Alaska, the Thule culture Eskimos in less than three centuries swept across the entire Arctic, absorbing or destroying the Dorsets. They crossed from Ellesmere Island to northern Greenland, moved southward along both the east and west coasts of Greenland, and spread south along the Labrador coast to the Strait of Belle Isle.

Superb hunters, the Thule Eskimos tackled all game, from seals, caribou, and walrus to the giant baleen whales of the Arctic seas. They had kayaks and sled dogs, and pursued the great whales in large, open skin-boats called umiaks. The Danish archeologist Count Eigil Knuth found the well-preserved wooden frame of a Thule umiak, dating from about 1500 A.D. in the easternmost part of Peary Land, less than five hundred miles from the North Pole.

In the early eighteenth century, Thule whale hunting declined and with it their distinctive way of life. Hunting sixty-foot whales with bone harpoons from skin-boats may have been a risky occupation, but one Greenland whale, sheathed in thirty tons of blubber, provided as much food as a thousand seals. Given this blubbery bounty, Thule people could afford to cluster in permanent villages with as many as thirty houses.

With the end of whaling, Thule culture ceased; the people dispersed, became more migratory, and the modern phase of Eskimo life began, with its tiny pockets of people scattered across the immensity of the Arctic. Similar in language and custom, in dress and mode of life, the Eskimos, who in their totality could easily fit into a large football stadium, were spread over the Arctic from eastern Siberia to the east coast of Greenland, and from Thule in northern Greenland to southern Labrador, distances of six thousand and two thousand miles respectively—equal to those from Capetown to Rome, and London to Moscow.

Of all the earth's regions, the Eskimos live in the harshest and most forbidding. Summers are short, cool, and mosquito-plagued, winters long, dark, and cold. The murderous climate and ever-present threat of famine could have turned the Eskimos into a glum and brooding people. Instead they are gay, gregarious, good-natured, and amazingly contented. Optimism and hope buoy them up in adversity. "The caribou will come!" they say and look south from the hills. Days pass. There is no more food in camp. "The caribou will come!" say the people, and when they do not come, they shrug resignedly, 'Ayornamat!—It can't be helped!" and they try to catch tomcod and ground squirrels to eke out an existence, because, surely, soon the caribou will come. Ekalun of Bathurst Inlet, recalling the days of his youth, said, "We worked hard then. We travelled much. If one was lucky, one had lots to eat. If one had no luck one was hungry. Often one was hungry. But then came again good times. And the people were happy and danced."

Innuit, the people, Eskimos proudly call themselves. Men pre-eminent, the Original Men to whom earth herself gave birth. For Indians and whites their legends postulate a less flattering ancestry. They are descended of an Eskimo girl who mated with a dog, human in appearance but vicious and monstrous inside.

Eskimo society in the past was one of equals. They acknowledged neither chiefs nor superiors, their language lacks the term. The closest they can come is to call a man *ishumata*—he who thinks, a man whom others respect for his wisdom. But power he had none. What power there was, lay within the community, in the rule of public opinion. The approval and esteem of other members of his group were a man's highest reward, ostracism his worst punishment.

Since Eskimos were an intensely social people, they generally tried to conform to the norms of behaviour of their society. But they were also a highly individualistic people, moody, impulsive, notoriously lacking in self-control and subject to sudden outbursts of passion. Murder, as a result, was fairly common. The Greenland ethnologist Knud Rasmussen once visited a fifteen-family community in the Coronation Gulf area of the central Arctic and found every grown man in this camp had been involved in at least one killing. In cases of quarrels and murders, the community did not intervene. Violent death, compensation for it, or revenge leading occasionally to protracted blood feuds, were the conern of the families involved. But if one person became too quarrelsome, too prone to commit murder, and generally a threat to the group's stability, it could decide his death. A person was then appointed to kill him.

Rasmussen tells of a case in which a man was designated by the community to execute his own brother. He looked upon it as a duty to be done, went to his brother, explained what had been decided and asked whether he preferred to be stabbed, strangled, or shot. The brother chose death by bullet and was

shot "without moving from where he was or exhibiting any sign of fear." I once lived with a gentle old man, kind, considerate, and courteous, who in his youth had killed two men for the sake of communal harmony. "It was necessary," he explained. "The men were no good. One had to kill them."

Warfare, on the other hand, the Eskimos did not know. For that they were neither sufficiently organized and civilized, nor did they have the reserves of food and leisure that would have permitted them to indulge in the luxury of protracted wars. They did fight sporadically with the Indians, from Alaska to Labrador, and the folklore of both peoples is replete with tales of mutual slaughter. But these were usually brief skirmishes, the result of chance encounters, conducted with a minimum of ritual and a maximum of efficiency.

The western idea of "chivalrous warfare" would have struck the pragmatic Eskimo as dumb and dangerous. His notion of battle was to sneak up to a sleeping Indian camp and massacre everyone in the shortest possible time and, when the chance presented itself, the Indians retaliated with similar attacks. But basically their choice of environment kept the antagonists apart: the northern Indians were a people of the forest; the Eskimos felt ill at ease among trees and preferred the tundra and the Arctic coasts.

One major cause of conflict in other societies, the concept of a family, a group, a tribe, or a nation having exclusive rights to a certain territory and its resources, did not exist among the Eskimos. The land and its wealth belonged to all. A man might leave his camp, join another group in its favourite hunting area, kill all the game he could, and everyone would be delighted with his success. Even the idea of tribal groupings was a very loose one among the Eskimos. People belonged to a certain area, rather than to tribes, and ties of kinship and acquaintance more than any formal organization held them together. The frequent word ending -*miut* (Aivilingmiut, Sadlermiut, Iglulingmiut) does not denote adherence to a tribe. It simply means "the people of" a certain place, similar to the "-er" in New Yorker or Montrealer. The people at North Camp on the Belcher Islands are known today as Companikumiut—the people who live where the (Hudson's Bay) Company is. On Southampton Island American servicemen during the Second World War called the area of the unsuitably shallow cove where they had to lighter their cargo ashore "Snafu," an army-navy slang acronym for "situation normal: all fouled up." The Eskimos who now live there are known as the Snafumiut.

The land of the Eskimos is not only climatically harsh, it is desperately poor in the raw materials most other societies consider essential to existence. Before the arrival of the white man, Eskimos had to rely on what materials were available to fashion their tools and implements. While a medieval English archer could quickly make a bow from the resilient wood of a yew tree, an Eskimo had to laboriously piece and peg his bow together from small, brittle fragments of driftwood. The fragile weapon had to be backed with a strip of sealskin and upon this lay the strong cords of plaited sinew that gave the bow its spring. Such a bow, made with simple stone tools from unsuitable material, may be a marvel of ingenuity, but it is still a poor weapon, and a hunter has to creep to within twenty paces of a caribou for a sure shot.

It took a month or more to fashion a cooking pot (looking like a miniature sarcophagus) from soapstone, chipping it out with a stone adze, and smoothing the pot by rubbing it with a harder stone. Where wood was unobtainable, pieces of caribou antler were straightened by soaking them in hot water, and the sections were pegged together to form harpoon and lance shafts. Fur clothes were sewn with needles made from the hard wingbones of gulls and geese, and thimbles were carved from muskox horn. Fire had to be made with a fire drill, or by striking chunks of pyrite together and catching the sparks in cottongrass or catkin fluff. Fox traps, certain types seven feet tall, were built of stones. Caribou pitfalls were dug into snowdrifts, covered with sheets of hard snow and baited with dog urine which caribou like for its salt content.

Nor were the best raw materials all to be found in one place. Long, laborious trips had to be made to obtain them. The people of Bathurst Inlet travelled to a valley two weeks away to obtain the very hard type of flint best suited to make bits for bow drills. Native copper, on the islands to the north, meant a week's trip; to get soapstone large enough to make pots required a three-week journey; and the great inland migration to the upper Thelon region to obtain wood for kayaks and sleds could last a year.

To cope with the endless work, there was a strict division of labour between the sexes. The men hunted, made all the weapons and most of the tools; the women cared for the children, cooked, cleaned skins, sewed all the clothes, and kept them in constant repair. Women rarely had trouble finding husbands since in most areas the best hunters would have two and, occasionally, three wives. Men also outnumbered women in those Eskimo groups practising infanticide, since it was invariably girls who were killed. This was the dictate not of a cruel people, but of a cruel environment. Infanticide was rare or unknown in the most game-rich regions inhabited by Eskimos, and most prevalent among the Netsilingmiut, who inhabited one of the harshest sections of the Arctic. Girls were strangled immediately after they were born to promote the maximum number of male births, of man-children who would grow up to be hunters and support their parents in their old age.

Rasmussen met a Netsilingmiut couple who had had twenty children. Of these ten little girls had been killed, four had died of disease, and one son had been killed in a kayak accident. Surviving were four sons and one daughter. Rasmussen asked them if they did not regret having killed so many girls and they said, "No, for without killing she would not have had so many children, and if she had had to suckle all the girls, who were born before the boys, she would have had no sons now."

Most Eskimos looked after their parents faithfully and honoured the aged. But when famine threatened, the old people had to die. They knew this, accepted it, and in some areas celebrated it with a party where all, including those about to die, were enjoying themselves. "For our custom up here is that all old people who can do no more, and whom death will not take, help death to take them. And they do this not merely to be rid of a life that is no longer a pleasure, but also to relieve their nearest relations of the trouble they give them," an Eskimo told Rasmussen.

Yet despite the severity of their lives, the threat of famine, the effort needed to produce even simple tools and weapons, and the strain upon each man when day after day he hunted unsuccessfully or when prolonged blizzards made it impossible to even attempt to hunt, the Eskimos were a gay, cheerful, contented people. They were masters in the art of Arctic survival, secure within their society, yet free as individuals. They were happy and hospitable. It was a hunter's pleasure to provide the most lavish feasts in the camp and to share the fruits of his skill and good fortune. His sole reward was the approbation of his equals.

It was, in many ways, a simple life, a basic life, concerned with the here and now, the enjoyment of each day and the happiness it brought. The Eskimos loved to travel, shrugged off its hardships and enjoyed its variety; they loved to visit and be visited, and to the men each day's hunt was a new challenge and a new adventure. Theirs was a closed economy. They imported nothing, exported nothing, knew no other people (except the despised Indians), and needed no other people. Each group, be it two families or ten, was entirely self-sufficient. They were masters of their own fate, and since they knew no others, they considered theirs the best of all possible worlds.

The advent of the white man's culture destroyed the fragile fabric of this ancient way of life. Its concepts of master and servant, of material wealth as a measure of a man's worth, of subordination of one man's wishes to another man's will, were alien and mystifying to the Eskimo mind. Even the European notion of life after death struck the Eskimos as odd. Why, they wondered, were only sinners admitted to such an obviously desirable place as a well-heated hell?

But there was no getting around the fact that the white men were possessors of marvellous things: steel needles, knives, files, iron pots, and, above all, guns and ammunition, things infinitely superior to anything the Eskimos had and guaranteed to make their existence easier. Knowledge of these goods bred desire, and desire unfulfilled bred discontent. But desire fulfilled resulted in dependence.

White men came to the Arctic to explore and exploit. Whalers from Scotland and New England pursued, and eventually nearly exterminated, the great bowhead whales both in the eastern and western Arctic. They sometimes used Eskimos to augment crews, but mainly they depended upon the natives to supply them with fresh meat: as much as fifty thousand pounds of caribou hindquarters and saddles (the Eskimos ate the rest) for five ships spending the winter of 1905 at Herschel Island in the western Arctic. And thousands of ships came to the north over the years. Muskoxen, easy to kill with guns since they do not flee, were hunted close to extinction; caribou were decimated; and when whales began to fail, whalers butchered the herds of walrus, white whales, and finally took out anything that could be sold back home.

In 1904, the whaler *Active* returned from Hudson Bay with a cargo consisting of two bowhead whales, sixty-nine white whales, thirty-eight walruses, fifty-two seals, thirty-two polar bear skins, 158 fox pelts, thirty muskox hides, one gyrfalcon, and fifteen tons of mica.

From the whalers, the Eskimos received guns, ammunition and various other goods they soon came to consider essential and, involuntarily, flotsam from the more than five hundred ships known to have been wrecked in Arctic waters.

The whalers destroyed much of the Arctic's wildlife wealth, the basis of Eskimo existence. And they left the Eskimos an evil legacy of mass starvation, disease, and dependence upon white man's goods. Bacteria do not flourish in cold. At the South Pole, scientists have only found one bacterium per pint of snow. The isolated Eskimos were an extremely hardy and healthy people, free of diseases. But their bodies lacked resistance to illnesses white men brought north, and rampant disease spread from camp to camp. Of the one thousand Eskimos in Alaska's Point Barrow region in 1828, less than one hundred survived in 1890; at Shishmaref Inlet where some two thousand Eskimos used to live on walrus and whale, only three families were left in 1890. Within two generations of contact with whites, ninety percent of the Mackenzie River Delta Eskimos had vanished; and fourteen years after they were "discovered" by the 1913-1918 Stefansson expedition, thirty percent of the Coronation Gulf Eskimos had died of influenza. In Labrador, where the Eskimo population dwindled from about 3,000 in 1750 to 750 in 1946, the Moravian Bishop Martin said in 1908: "The wish of all of us is that the work of our Church here may be maintained until the dying hour of the Eskimo race has arrived, or until the last remnants of the race are absorbed by the [white] Settler populations." In 1956, 1,600 Eskimos suffering from tuberculosis were in hospitals in southern Canada, one-sixth of Canada's entire Eskimo population!

After the whalers, came the traders and, in their wake, the missionaries (the H.B.C. initials of the Hudson's Bay Company are ironically interpreted as "Here Before Christ"). Eskimo life changed from subsistence hunting to a trading economy based on the pelts of Arctic fox, a commodity subject to the cyclic fluctuations of fox populations and the caprice of fashion. Prices spiralled to $63 for white and $250 for blue foxes in 1929, slumped during the Depression to $8 and less, and fell to an all-time low of $3 per pelt after the Second World War.

Early winter, traditionally, had been a time when Eskimos met in larger groups. Fall hunting and fishing were finished, the ice not yet suitable for seal hunting, and the Eskimos danced and sang, told stories and played games. It was the most social time of an essentially sociable people. Trapping

changed this pattern. Families dispersed to their trap lines, groups were even more fragmented than before, old bonds were weakened, traditions died, the Eskimos' ancient autarky ceased, and their dependence upon white man's goods and, occasionally, white man's assistance increased.

After the Second World War, the Cold War came to the Arctic. In a flurry of activity, D.E.W. (Distant Early Warning) Line stations were built across the top of the continent. Eskimos left ancient hunting grounds to work as labourers, but when their services were no longer required, they often lacked the will and resilience to go back to the land. They settled in tents and shacks near the sites or in the slowly developing settlements—an incipient Arctic proletariat, bereft of their old culture yet not belonging to a new one either.

The establishment in Canada of government services, schools, hospitals, and administration offices in the settlements and, eventually, the provision of good housing in the villages, plus subtle and not-so-subtle pressure to abandon camp life, resulted in the concentration of nearly all Eskimos in settlements. The people of the smaller communities still lead mainly a hunting-trapping life and, in some areas, return "to the land" for a few weeks in summer. The people in many of the larger settlements exist primarily on welfare. Until the development of the Arctic provides them with work, and until their education has sufficiently advanced to enable them to compete successfully with whites, they dwell in an unhappy hybrid state: emotionally linked to their ancient hunting culture which is now dead, and not yet part and partners of the white man's Arctic world with its material compensations and the status symbols of its stratified society for which the young in particular yearn.

Far from this new Eskimo existence with its problems and its promise, another form of life continues, that of the last camp Eskimos, specks of isolated humanity here and there in the vastness of the Arctic, leading a vanishing way of life. These camps exist for various reasons—geographic isolation; an administrative oversight; a game-rich area—but mainly because these people prefer the emotional security of their traditional way of life, to which over thousands of years they have become so superbly adapted. Like a vanishing species, they are avidly studied by scientists, to the extent that it has been said the typical present-day camp family consists of a man, a wife, three children, and an anthropologist. The more accessible groups are in fact overrun by thesis-seeking scientists; one camp in Alaska became somewhat hostile after it was visited by forty-five anthropologists within one year.

Apart from these fairly unwelcome visits, camp life continues according to the immutable rules governing a hunting people in the Arctic: to take from each season what each season brings; to share your food with all members of the group, as they will share theirs with you; to rise to superhuman efforts when the hunt requires it, and to live in quiet harmony with yourself and others when bad weather imprisons you in your tent; to do as you like and let others do as they like (this is perhaps the hardest precept for a white man to follow, so used are we to impose upon others while others impose upon us).

One of the last and largest camp areas in Canada is Bathurst Inlet in the central Arctic, inhabited by eighty-nine people living in eleven widely scattered camps. In winter they hunt seal at the breathing holes and fish through the ice. In spring, the caribou come from the taiga in the south across the vastness of the tundra to the Arctic shores. In summer the men fish; in fall the seals are fat and float when shot, the new clove-brown fur of the caribou is short and strong, ideal for winter clothes, and the animals are heavy and fat after pasturing all summer on the Arctic meadows. Fat char ascend the rivers and ground squirrels, ready for their eight-month winter sleep, look like fat, furred sausages with feet. It is the time to collect meat, fat, and fish for the dark, lean months of winter ahead.

Camp life is hard, infinitely harder than life in a settlement where Eskimos now have well-heated, three-bedroom houses, electricity, and often washing machines, refrigerators, and other amenities people in the south take for granted. It is an unpredictable life. One year spring comes, but the caribou do not. The people travel far, work hard, and find nothing. They may have to trap ground squirrels to subsist. The dogs become weak; travelling is curtailed. Another year, large numbers of caribou stay near the camps all year, seals are plentiful, life is relatively easy. To endure and succeed in such a life, a hunter must be resourceful and hardy, he must have faith in himself, a lot of optimism, a certain fatalism, and the ability to live each day and enjoy the good it brings and not spoil it with worry about the morrow.

And yet, there is only
One great thing,
The only thing:
To live;
To see in huts and on journeys
The great day that dawns,
And the light that fills the world.

WINTER

The Eskimo language has more than a hundred words for various types of snow, and a nearly equal number to describe different ice formations. During eight to nine months of the year, snow covers the Arctic land, and ice its seas. The plant growing season in the high Arctic is forty days or less, and about eighty days on the Arctic mainland. Certain lichens survive in regions so rugged and cold that they may only be able to grow during one day of the year. A small patch of lichen may be hundreds of years old.

Cold typifies the Arctic, and the ability to survive it typifies the plants and animals that inhabit it. Its ultimate test is the deadly combination of wind and cold: a twenty-mile-an-hour wind at zero degrees Fahrenheit produces greater heat loss than −40° F. temperatures and no wind. Yet muskoxen, large (up to nine hundred pounds) herbivores, live on northern Ellesmere Island, where the average January temperature is −30° F. and February is about as cold. Temperatures can drop to −50° and even −65°, and storms last for days. The sun sets on October 22 and does not rise again above the horizon until March 1. But rather than seek shelter in the valleys, muskoxen move in winter to the wind-lashed slopes, where thin snow cover makes it easier to reach the sparse vegetation. The cold, it seems, does not bother them. It may be −60° outside, within himself the muskox maintains a comfortable internal climate of 101° F. To prevent heat loss and death from exposure, the muskox is wrapped in a thick, silky-soft layer of wool, called *qiviut* by the Eskimos, and carries above it an immense cloak of coarse guard hairs reaching nearly to the ground.

Twelve hundred miles further south, at the edge of the northern forest belt, it can be as cold as on Ellesmere Island, but on extremely cold days, when temperatures plummet to −60°, it is usually completely calm. Sounds carry far in the still Arctic air, and sound waves are reflected by low cloud cover. Caribou walking a mile away can be heard distinctly, and they can be seen from afar since clouds of steam hover above the herds, and a running animal leaves a frozen vapour trail.

Like muskoxen, caribou rely on an extremely thick fur to protect them from the searing cold. The hairs of the new fall fur are short, dense, and a rich clove-brown. They grow throughout fall and winter, both in length and thickness, pushing against each other until they stand erect, a deep-pile carpet of fur an inch to an inch and a half thick and so efficient as an insulating layer that caribou seem impervious to cold.

The long-legged caribou, its arch-enemy the Arctic wolf, and several other Arctic mammals maintain two internal temperatures: the one in the extremities may be fifty degrees lower than that of the body. The legs are just warm enough to avoid frostbite, yet cool enough to keep heat loss to a minimum.

Some Arctic birds, like the ptarmigan and the Arctic owl, have well-protected, densely feathered feet. In others, like the raven and the Arctic gulls, an intricate internal thermostat keeps the temperature in their naked legs just above the freezing point, while their body temperature is nearly seventy degrees higher.

The aquatic mammals of the Arctic have a special problem. Although the water temperature in winter remains fairly steady at 28° F., heat conduction in water is about 250 times greater than in air. Their protection against the sapping chill of icy water is fat, an excellent insulating medium. Wrapped in a blubber blanket, two to four inches thick on the smaller seals and nearly two feet thick on the great Greenland whale, the marine mammals of the Arctic have no trouble being warm in cold water. But when seals and walrus haul out on land in summer, their blubber-encased bodies are in danger of overheating. Then a network of blood vessels opens towards the body surface, blood courses along, under, and within the skin, is cooled, and circulates inward to cool the body. At such times, the usually madder-brown walrus turns a bright pink and, as one scientist has put it, "when you see a walrus blush, you know that he is hot."

Cold the Arctic animals do not fear; nature has magnificently equipped them to withstand it. But sudden temperature fluctuations can be disastrous to them. Until the 1880s, caribou were numerous on the Belcher Islands in eastern Hudson Bay. One year, a great amount of snow fell, covering valleys and dells between the rock ridges with a five- and six-foot layer. In March, the weather suddenly turned mild. It rained and the snow turned to mush. Abruptly the wind veered, gales struck the islands from the north, and the water-logged snow turned into a hard, glittering ice shield. The caribou scraped and scratched in vain. Since they could not reach the lichen below, they starved and died out on the Belcher Islands.

Warm foehn winds in midwinter are the curse of Greenland. Sheep farmers in southwest Greenland fear warm winter wind and rain, because the wool of their animals becomes soaked with water. When it turns cold and the sheep lie down, they freeze to the ground and starve. Caribou have died out in east Greenland (and the wolves who depended upon them for food), and muskoxen have become rare in this region. All three were the victims not of cold, but of sudden, deadly warmth in winter.

When it is intensely cold, birds ruffle their feathers to trap more air, mammals fluff out their fur, and men have goose pimples in a pathetic vestigial attempt to raise a protective hair covering they no longer possess. As the naked descendant of warm-weather anthropoids, man is singularly unsuited for life in the Arctic. Nor has he been long enough in the north to become physically adapted to its rigours, as are the animals that inhabit it. Yet some northern tribes seem to have a remarkable ability to endure cold. Siberia's Yakuts sleep contentedly at −60° in a lean-to heated only by a small fire. Eskimo children play naked and without apparent discomfort on the sleeping platform of a chilly igloo. Near the other end of the world, the now nearly extinct subantarctic Fuegians show a similar capacity to withstand cold, as noted already by Charles Darwin: "A woman, who was suckling a recently born child, came one day alongside the vessel [H.M.S. *Beagle*], and remained there out of sheer curiosity, whilst the sleet fell and thawed on her naked bosom, and the skin of her naked baby!'' The anthropologist Diamond Jenness tells of an Eskimo woman who, during a ''howling north-west gale'' at a temperature of −29° F., ''withdrew her tiny baby from under her jacket and leisurely changed its sole garment, a diaper of caribou fur.'' More often an Eskimo baby sits completely naked in the voluminous hood of its mother's fur amautik. Even if the temperature is −40°, at the slightest sign that something is about to happen, the mother extracts the baby in all haste from its cozy nest and holds it out over the snow.

The Eskimos are known for their ''warm hands.'' This, it seems, is due to a slight modification of blood vessels in the hands permitting a better circulation of warming blood. Although one tends to think of Eskimos as flat-nosed, they are in fact the most narrow-nosed people on earth, a physical adaptation, some scientists think, to the extreme cold and dryness of the Arctic air.

If such physical modifications are in fact the result of incipient adaptation, they are still very minor. Any white man using Eskimo clothing and survival techniques can endure the murderous climate as well as a native. This has been amply demonstrated by explorers like Stefansson and Freuchen. Matthew Henson, the man who accompanied Peary to the North Pole, was a Negro and, being dressed Eskimo fashion, seems to have been as warm as the Eskimos who accompanied the expedition.

Thus man's ability to live in the Arctic is not due to any physiological changes, but to cultural adaptation and specialization. It is not his ability to withstand great cold but his knowledge of how to protect himself against it that has made the Eskimo master of the Arctic.

An Eskimo caught in a blinding blizzard at sub-zero temperatures in an area where he can't build an igloo, brushes the snow off a stone, sits down with his back to the wind, leans forward, and waits until the storm is over, a day or more if necessary. He may even sleep, secure in the knowledge that his superb, double-layered suit of caribou skin clothing will keep him from freezing.

A complete set of Eskimo winter clothing consists of inner and outer boots, inner and outer parkas, fur pants, and mittens. The inner clothes are worn with the fur towards the skin, the outer suit with the fur outside. The pants are baggy and held tight by a drawstring around the waist. Inner and outer parkas are loose-fitting garments, but a ruff of fur (preferably wolverine) around the inner and outer hoods and a snug fit around the neck and shoulders prevent warm air from escaping. The clothing thus takes maximum advantage of the basic principle that warm air does not move downwards. A complete Eskimo winter outfit weighs about ten pounds and will keep the wearer comfortably warm at −40°. Comparable clothing made of southern materials weighs thirty pounds and over, and is more cumbersome and less warm.

In some areas, as on the Belcher Islands where caribou have died out, the Eskimos, bereft of the best clothing material the Arctic offers, use ingenious substitutes. On the Belcher Islands, Eskimo women make parkas of eider duck skins. Such a *mitvin* is heavier and more fragile than a caribou parka, but as warm.

The principle that warm air does not escape downwards was also used by Eskimos of former days in building their houses. The entrance was low, and one had to creep through a ''cold trap'' passage up into the house. If the door was closed, this was mainly to keep the ravenous dogs out. The warmth in the building, created by the inhabitants' body heat and the burning seal-oil lamps, stayed in the house and, since warm air is lighter than cold air, did not escape through the low entrance passage.

In Alaska and Greenland Eskimos built their winter houses of sod, stones, bones, or driftwood, and used igloos mainly as convenient shelters on hunting trips. Only in the central Arctic did the Eskimos live all winter in igloos. (*Igloo*, incidentally, means house in Eskimo—any house, from a sod hut to Buckingham Palace. *Igloovigaq* is a snow-house.) An igloo is quickly built (two men can construct an igloo spacious enough for five people in about an hour), and one seal-oil lamp burning steadily keeps the temperature reasonably comfortable. After a while the interior becomes glazed, the walls drip, and the igloo turns from a cozy snow-house into a chilly ice-house. Then a new igloo has to be built. For dance festivals, the Copper Eskimos built igloos large enough to hold a hundred people, and until recently the Eskimos of Pelly Bay constructed at Christmastime a super-igloo, its vast vaulted roof supported by interior snow pillars, spacious enough for the entire community to crowd in for midnight mass.

But the north is changing fast. When a Canadian Eskimo boy recently visited a southern school, the teacher asked the children to draw a typical Eskimo scene. All the white children made pictures of igloos and sled dogs. The Eskimo boy's drawing showed a house and a skidoo.

White men's tales from the Arctic often read like long, depressing weather reports. Cold is their enemy, warmth the goal of their dreams. Eskimo stories, now as well as in the past, rarely deal with cold. Cold they conquered through cultural adaptation, and unless it impeded hunting, weather played a very minor role in Eskimo stories and conversation. Food, or the lack of it, was the all-engrossing subject, the Eskimos' major preoccupation in life. Heaven they imagined as a place where ''caribou graze in great herds, and they are easy to hunt,'' and in hell people ''are always hungry, for their only food is butterflies.''

The great fear was famine:

> Hard times, dearth times
> Plague us every one,
> Stomachs are shrunken,
> Dishes are empty.

The great joy was food:

Know you the smell
Of pots on the boil?
And lumps of blubber
Slapped down on the side bench?
Aja–ja–japape
Hu–hue! Joyfully
Greet we those,
who brought us plenty!

Food was shared. "Among the people, no man will lack for a meal as long as there is food. It is the custom of the people," an Eskimo told a missionary on the Labrador coast. Good hunters consistently fed hunters less skilled and energetic and their families. Inept hunters, particularly if they were considered lazy were occasionally lampooned in songs and held up to public ridicule, but in general the Eskimo did not use the term "a poor hunter." There were "lucky hunters" and "unlucky hunters," and they believed that "luck nearly always follows after misfortune. If this were not so, people would soon die out."

Often luck ran out, and the people died. "Life is so with us that we are never surprised when we hear someone has starved to death. We are so used to it," a Netsilik Eskimo told Rasmussen.

The last resort was cannibalism. The Eskimos had a horror of it, but condoned it. Life must go on.

"When my father was a young man," an old Eskimo in a settlement on Hudson Strait told me, "he and his mother were caught in a famine. The people died in camp and they left to reach another camp, hoping to find food there. They travelled and starved. They ate the dogs, the sealskin thongs, and part of their clothing. When there was nothing left, my grandmother told my father, 'Now you must eat me. You are young and will have children. I am old and will not live much longer anyway.' They built an igloo, and he strangled his mother and ate her. And that is how my father survived."

Rasmussen tells of a Netsilik mother who gave birth during a famine. She strangled the child, froze it, and ate it. The next day a seal was caught, and she survived the famine.

It has been suggested by some anthropologists that the Eskimo's wonderful capacity for happiness and gaiety was a form of psychological defence mechanism which enabled him to survive mentally unimpaired in this land without pity. An Eskimo expressed the same thought when he told Rasmussen: "Oh! You strangers only see us happy and free of care. But if you knew the horrors we often have to live through, you would understand too why we are so fond of laughing, why we love food and song and dancing. There is not one among us but has experienced a winter of bad hunting, when many people starved to death around us and when we ourselves only pulled through by accident."

In winter, the Eskimo's life in most regions of the Arctic depended upon seal. Where hunters lived in reasonable distance of open water, seals were hunted at the floe edge, the limit of landfast ice. Even in the severest winters and in the

highest Arctic there are extensive areas of open water, called *polynias*, a word derived from the Russian *polyi* meaning open. When travelling over sea ice in winter, one can see open water a great distance away. A dull greyish pall hovers over it near the horizon, the reflection upon the sky of the sea's dark colour. Sailors called it "water sky," as opposed to "iceblink," the whitish glare in the sky that indicates extensive icefields.

To a white man the floe edge seems sinister. At −40°, the sea water is about sixty-eight degrees warmer than the surrounding air and it literally steams. Peary, coming upon open water in −50° weather, wrote that in the bitter cold there rose from the sea, "inky clouds of vapour which gathered in a sullen canopy overhead."

The floe edge is not permanent. A storm can break it and roll it back hundreds of yards. And on a calm, intensely cold night, it can "grow" out into the sea for a mile or more. While slowly freezing sea ice has a salinity of about two per mill, fast frozen sea ice may have a salinity of twenty per mill. Increased salinity gives ice greater tensile strength and at the fast-freezing floe edge the sea ice's tensile strength may be twice that of fresh-water ice.

It is an eerie, uncanny place. The water smokes in the bitter cold. The ice, in places only two inches thick, bends and buckles as dogs and sled pass over it. The hunter hides behind a block of snow or ice. He scrapes the ice with his harpoon shaft, back and forth, back and forth, for hours on end. The grating noise travels far in water and attracts the curious seal. As the seal surfaces, the hunter whistles and makes strange mewing noises to lure the animal within range of his harpoon. Hours pass, an entire day passes. Patiently the hunter waits. His fate and that of his family depends upon his ability to concentrate his entire being on this one task—to kill a seal, to spend a day, and two and three, if necessary, crouched behind the block of ice and to hurl the harpoon in one lightning-quick movement when a seal bobs up within range.

Tremendous endurance and infinite patience enabled the Eskimo hunter to succeed. Tests carried out by the U.S. army show that the ratio of physical fitness between the average Eskimo, a highly trained Arctic army soldier, and the average airman is in the order of 3.5 : 2.5 : 1. Akeeagok, an Ellesmere Island Eskimo whom I accompanied on a spring polar-bear hunt, once pursued a bear on foot through a vast area of chaotically piled up pressure ice. He ran without pause for nearly seven hours. And he didn't get the bear.

Until the recent introduction of polar bear quotas and the use of motor toboggans, the Eskimos of the eastern and western Arctic hunted the mighty bears with dogs to hold them at bay. In the central Arctic, food was often scarce, Eskimos had few dogs, and when a man sighted a polar bear, he pursued it alone and on foot, armed only with a fragile bone lance or harpoon. He ran, sometimes for whole days, until the bear stopped and turned. Then the man with his puny weapon faced the bear, a bear so powerful he can kill an eight-hundred-pound bearded seal with one blow of his long-clawed paw.

Many a hunter has been killed or crippled in these encounters.

As soon as ice begins to form in fall, the ringed seal of the Arctic gnaws breathing holes through the ice. As the ice thickens, the seals continue to gnaw and scrape to keep these breathing holes, called *agloos* by the Eskimos, open as vital vents to the air above, sometimes through ice six feet thick. Each seal has from four to a dozen or more breathing holes, and by surfacing in those of his neighbours he can even further extend his range. When a polar bear finds an agloo, he scrapes the snow away and lies in wait, for hours and sometimes for days, until the seal surfaces in this hole to breathe. With one mighty swipe of his paw the bear pins the luckless pinniped against the agloo's icy wall, grabs its head nearly simultaneously with his powerful teeth, and yanks the seal upward through the constricted hole with such force that its bones buckle and break.

The Eskimos, too, wait at the agloos for seal to surface. From Greenland to Siberia, since times immemorial, Eskimo hunters have hovered over seal breathing holes in winter, waiting endlessly, patiently. Because the seal is life.

In the central Arctic where there are no walrus or whales, agloo hunting has become most highly developed. But now only a few "camp Eskimos" practise this ancient hunt. For them, survival in this region depends on their skill and success in finding and capturing the seals. Specially trained dogs find the agloos. The hunter cuts the top layer of snow with his snow knife and carefully lifts it out. With a long, slender, curved probe of caribou antler, he examines the exact shape of the breathing hole so he will know how to thrust his harpoon. A special spoon, carved from muskox horn, is used to remove every particle of snow and ice that has fallen onto the water and could warn the seal. The snow is then replaced and a long sliver of bone or wood, the *idlak*, is inserted through the snow into the agloo. As the seal surfaces to breathe, it will push against the tip of the idlak and alert the hunter above. To muffle even the slightest sound, the man spreads a piece of thick caribou winter fur on the snow, steps on it, and freezes into immobility, bent forward like a three-quarter-closed jackknife, or he sits on his haunches, his harpoon at the ready, his entire being riveted upon the little coloured feather on top of his idlak. When it moves, he must strike.

The hunter waits, motionless like a statue. It is −40°. The wind whispers across the endless expanse of snow and ice. The hunter waits. Hour after hour. "I have heard of a man who spent two and a half days at a breathing hole, sometimes standing, sometimes sitting, but awake all the time," Rasmussen tells. When, finally, the seal comes and the idlak jiggles, the hunter drives the harpoon through the snow into the seal below in one smooth powerful motion. Or, after waiting for hours, he misses.

Ekalun of Bathurst Inlet stood over an agloo for four hours, and then missed the surfacing seal because an ice chip deflected the harpoon from its true aim. "*Mamiena*—it is not good," he said laconically and started to look for a new agloo to resume the frigid vigil for seal.

The Eskimo is most admirable in adversity. He does not curse (his language is practically devoid of swear words) or rant or rave; he does not brood over past failure and the misfortune it has brought him. He does not rebel against fate; he accepts it. "*Mamiena*," he says, "it is not good," or "*Ayornamat*–it can't be helped."

Early winter is the Eskimos' time of ease–provided he has food. The caribou have left, the caches are filled with meat, fish, and great tallow-like slabs of caribou backfat. The ice is not yet suitable for seal hunting and, in the past, a taboo prohibited seal hunting in many areas until the women had finished sewing the winter fur clothes. The men slept, told stories, played games, or danced and sang–each man singing songs which were his own property. He, and he alone, was allowed to sing them, though some songs were shared by a group and even passed from group to group.

In January and February, agloo hunting begins in the murky, colourless twilight of the winter days. Seal means food and warmth. The high-calorie blubber gives strength and endurance to the people. Burning in their crescent-shaped seal-oil lamps, blubber heats the homes, cooks the meals and, even more important, melts fresh-water ice or snow into drinking water. Lack of blubber means hunger, icy, dark homes, and excruciating thirst. Although Eskimos are hardy and inured to cold, their exclusive fat-meat diet of former days may have helped them to withstand the rigours of winter. Recent studies have shown that a high-protein diet raises basal metabolism and can increase the body's heat production by as much as fifteen percent.

Early European voyages to the Arctic, with men living primarily on a fat-meat-starch diet, all boiled or fried, were haunted by scurvy. Sixty-one of Jens Munk's sixty-four-member crew died of scurvy in one winter (1619–1620) near the mouth of the Churchill River on the west coast of Hudson Bay. In 1837, the Arctic whaler *Dee* returned to Aberdeen with nine alive of a crew of forty-six, and the whaler *Advice* to Dundee with seven survivors of a crew of forty-nine. And all 129 officers and men of Sir John Franklin's 1845 expedition perished of scurvy and starvation in an area where Eskimos with infinitely poorer weapons had lived for millennia.

Where white men died of scurvy, Eskimos lived in excellent health on a diet consisting nearly exclusively of fat, meat, and fish.

More than any people on earth, the early Eskimos were independent of plants and vegetables. In spring and summer in most areas, they ate some plants: the roots of vetch; the leaves of sorrel; and the stems of roseroot. The Eskimos of east Greenland were so fond of seaweed and ate it in such quantities that they are thought to have derived fifty percent of their vitamin C requirement from it. Most Eskimos gathered berries in fall (but rarely made an attempt to store them) and a mixture of whipped blubber and cloudberries is known in Alaska as "Eskimo ice cream." They even had a type of chewing gum made of solidified seal oil and willow catkins.

Some vegetable food was obtained second-hand. Nearly all Eskimos regarded the slightly fermented, sourish contents of the caribou and muskox paunch as a delicacy. Partly digested willow buds from ptarmigan gizzard and intestine were highly esteemed. But if vegetables were eaten, it was mainly as a welcome change to the somewhat monotonous meat menu. It was not a necessity. The Polar Eskimos of northwestern Greenland, and some of the Central Eskimos hardly ever ate any vegetable matter at all.

The vitamins these Eskimos required to keep healthy, they obtained by eating much of the meat, fat, and intestines raw, a habit to which they owe their name—the word "Eskimo" is derived from an opprobrious Algonquian Indian term meaning "eaters of raw meat." Many of the animal parts Eskimos consider delicacies (and white men consider revolting) are particularly rich in vitamins: the raw skin of white whale and narwhal, called *muktuk* by the Eskimos, contains as much vitamin C per unit of weight as oranges; raw seal liver holds many vitamins, especially A and D (polar bear and bearded seal liver contain so much vitamin A they are poisonous, and people eating them can die of hypervitaminosis); the sweetish, rubbery seal intestines and seal stomachs crammed with partly digested shrimp tasting like lobster paste are the culinary climax of a real Eskimo feast, and both happen to be particularly rich in vitamins.

Since Eskimo dogs were as carnivorous as their masters, they were direct competitors for available food. Rasmussen, during his stay with the Netsilik Eskimos found even the best hunters rarely succeeded in killing more than thirty seals in one long winter and spring. This was barely enough to feed their families and those of less fortunate hunters. To keep and feed large dog teams would have meant near-starvation for men and dogs. Yet dogs were essential to winter travel, and throughout the Eskimos' immense range, the number of dogs kept by each group was a fair indicator of the region's food supply. Wherever the Eskimos hunted large sea mammals, walrus or whales, as in northwestern Greenland, northern Hudson Bay, Baffin Island, or parts of Alaska, large dog teams, fairly well fed, hauled their masters with speed and ease. In the central Arctic where food was scarce, men and especially women toiled in harness, assisted by one or two dogs.

The dog was man's first domestic animal. Sometime in the Mesolithic Period, man adopted dog–or dog adopted man. (Scientists are not quite sure which party made the first overtures to promote this lasting relationship.) According to the famous Austrian ethologist Konrad Lorenz, these first dogs were small and jackal-like. When man first came to the Arctic, "It was evidently found desirable to introduce as much wolf as possible into the strain" to give the dogs more stamina and strength. The result was the husky: cheerful, powerful, and incredibly hardy.

In the eastern Arctic the usual sled load is about one hundred pounds per dog. An eight-dog team will haul the heavy sled, plus eight hundred pounds, for thirty or forty miles per day over reasonably good ice. But if they are pushed and the load is not quite so heavy, they can cover, with little rest, one hundred miles and more in twenty-four hours.

Given the chance, a husky (like a wolf) can gulp down an incredible amount of food, as much as ten to fifteen pounds of meat. Normally, working dogs receive a pound of meat and a quarter pound of fat (blubber or tallow) per day, but often they receive little or nothing and even then they will faithfully haul the sled for many days. When the explorer David T. Hanbury crossed the Canadian Barrens in 1902, hunting once was poor and the dogs received no food for five days. But his Eskimo companions did not worry. "They said that [the dogs] might be unfed for ten days and still be able to haul, and that they would not die of starvation for a long time."

The dog sled was made of wood where available. The low, broad runners and the cross-slats were lashed together with sealskin thongs to make the sled extremely flexible, an essential feature when travelling across the furrowed, fluted, hard Arctic snow, so compacted by winter gales that a ten-ton tractor leaves a track only an inch or two deep.

The sled runners were shod with whale bone, or strips of caribou antler were laboriously pegged to the wood. In the central Arctic, Eskimos dug up peaty earth in fall with a special curved mattock made of caribou antler. In winter the earth was boiled into thick paste, and the hot mud-pack spread evenly on the runners where it froze stone-hard. Before every trip, the runners were coated with ice. Snow was soaked in warm water, the resultant mush spread onto the runners, planed smooth with a scraper or snow knife, and coated by dipping a piece of polar bear skin into lukewarm water and running it quickly over the runner, giving it an even, smooth glaze. This reduced friction to a minimum and enabled the dogs to haul the heavy sled.

Driftwood was plentiful in some regions of the Arctic. Washed down the great rivers of Siberia and North America, massive tree trunks were carried far by Arctic currents, and sometimes pushed into bulwark-like masses by ice on some remote beaches of the far north. Remnants of the bark *Jeannette*, abandoned by the American 1879 expedition under Lieutenant DeLong north of Siberia, were found three years later near the southern tip of Greenland. But in some parts of the central Arctic, particularly in the Gulf of Boothia, driftwood was so rare it was the subject of Eskimo myths. The small wood pieces that they occasionally found came from forests underneath the sea, the Netsilingmiut believed. Among them, a piece of wood was worth a wife, and the most energetic and venturesome travelled overland as far as the Thelon River to obtain wood for sleds and kayaks. Sometimes the trip lasted several years.

When all the usual raw materials for sled building (wood, whale bones, ivory, baleen, horn, or bone) were lacking, the ingenious Eskimos could still construct a sled. They shaped runners out of soaked seal, caribou, or muskox hides. Frozen solid, they kept their shape until the first thaw. Frozen fish or frozen strips of meat were used as cross-bars. These sleds could carry several hundred pounds and had one advantage over other conveyances: in times of dearth the sled could be eaten.

In much of the Arctic, motor toboggans are now replacing the faithful but voracious husky. The four hundred sled dogs at Coral Harbour on Southampton Island in Hudson Bay annually devour about 115,000 pounds of meat and 36,000 pounds of fat. In this region, where Eskimos hunt both walrus and white whales, it is fairly easy to procure such a mountain of meat. In other areas, where these bulk-food animals are rare or missing, Eskimos have to spend an inordinate amount of time hunting seals to feed their dogs.

In the most isolated regions of the Arctic, as at Bathurst Inlet, sled dogs are now, as in the past, the sole form of winter transportation and are used for brief hunting trips as well as for long migrations in search of seal and fish and caribou.

A travelling Eskimo is the most observant of human beings. On his mind he imprints a myriad of details—an odd-shaped rock, a distinctive patch of lichen, the loom of a distant cliff—and years later when travelling through the same region, these small landmarks, nearly instinctively remembered, will guide him. He knows the prevailing winds, knows their direction and can read their message in the wavelike ripples of the *sastrugi*, the hard snow ridges sculpted by winter's winds. They guide him safely through the skim-milk haze of a whiteout that destroys a person's depth perception to such an extent that one explorer mistook a three-inch lemming for an eight-hundred-pound muskox. The Eskimo travels with assurance through this wintry land of white, and cold, and wind. He and his ancestors for thousands of years have learned to live with winter and with cold. To white men the Arctic in winter is a harsh, hostile, barren, forbidding land. To the Eskimo it is home.

Hard times, dearth times
Plague us every one,
Stomachs are shrunken,
Dishes are empty.

Below: A husky peers through a snow mask. In a blizzard, the sled dogs curl up and let the snow bury them. No matter how cold it is, Eskimos never take their dogs inside.

Right: At daybreak, an Eskimo prepares for a trip. A piece of skin is frequently dipped into lukewarm water, and run back and forth across the broad runners of the sled until they are coated with a smooth, even glaze.

A lonely Eskimo dog team crosses the vastness of Bathurst Inlet. Once dog teams were the Eskimo's only means of winter transportation. Now, they are increasingly being replaced by motor toboggans. Only in the smaller, more isolated settlements and in the last camps do Eskimos still use dog teams in winter.

For the camp children, the white realm of the north is one vast playground. Warmly dressed and ever active, they do not mind the cold. Except during a storm, they play outside from early morning until late at night, chasing each other and romping in the snow.

Above: Clad in double-layered caribou-skin clothes, a little Eskimo boy is nearly impervious to the cold. Besides, Eskimo children are hardy. Tiny tots crawl lightly clad around the sleeping platform in the chilly tent; older children play outside all winter regardless of cold. Only a storm will keep them inside.

Left: Exhausted from playing, a fur-clad boy sleeps on a sled. He wears the practical pants Eskimo mothers make for their children, with a fur-flanked opening in the rear. When the children stand, the flap is closed. When nature calls, they stoop and the flap opens.

Polar bear hunting has been made much easier and less dangerous by the use of guns. In former days, the Eskimos attacked polar bears with lances. Trained huskies play an important part in the hunt even now. They hold the polar bear at bay, thus enabling the hunter to come within shooting range. The dogs harass the mighty bear when he runs, and jump nimbly aside when the bear turns upon them in fury or tries to swat and bite his pursuers.

Nanook – the great white bear – is dead.

At the end of the day, a long line of Eskimo dog teams pulls toward their evening rest.

Given snow of the right consistency and a long-bladed snow knife, an Eskimo is assured of a comfortable, wind-proof shelter, wherever evening may find him in the Arctic. An igloo is built in a continuous spiral of snow blocks weighing between forty and fifty pounds. As the walls rise, the inward bevel of each block is increased. A large, fitted cap-block placed on the top finishes the structure.

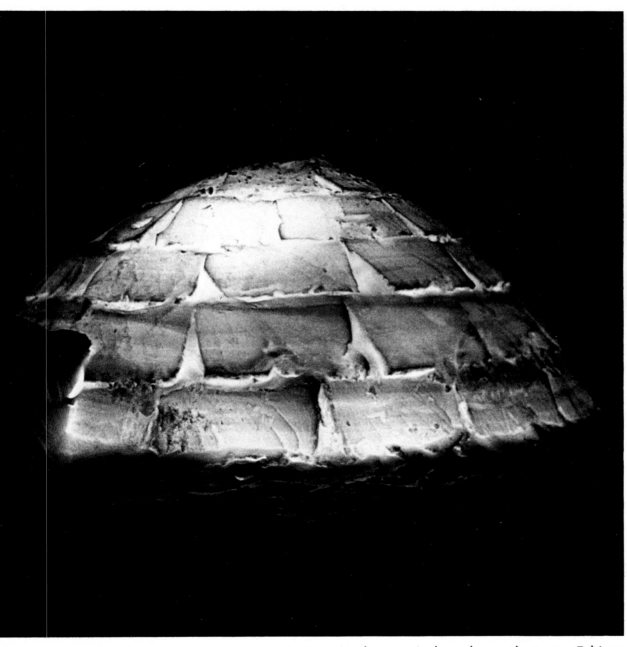

Secure from wind and weather, an Eskimo hunter sleeps peacefully in his igloo. Since the dry Arctic snow is hygroscopic, the igloo, for one day at least, can be comfortably heated. The snow blocks will absorb the moisture for that length of time; after that the walls become glazed and drip.

With two trained dogs on a long leash, an Eskimo hunter sets out to search for agloos, the breathing holes of seals, hidden under the snow. The hunter cuts the snow away, carefully inspects the position of the breathing hole, replaces the snow sheet, and inserts through it a long, thin sliver of wood called an idlak. When the seal rises in the breathing hole, it pushes against the idlak, and the hunter thrusts his harpoon through the snow into the seal.

Motionless, an agloo hunter waits above the snow-hidden breathing hole of a seal. He stands on a thick piece of caribou skin to muffle even the slightest sound. Hunters stand like this for hours, occasionally for an entire day, in one instance for more than twenty-four hours, waiting for the seal when it surfaces.

Left: A successful hunter hauls the harpooned seal from the enlarged agloo. Right: An Eskimo woman cuts up the seal her husband has brought back from a successful hunt. Meat and blubber are buried in the snow to serve as food for men and dogs when needed. The blood is carefully collected and later made into blood soup, a rich food that Eskimos love.

SPRING

Geographers define a desert as "any area with an annual rainfall of less than ten inches." According to this definition, nearly the entire Arctic is a desert—a cold desert. The average annual precipitation on Ellesmere Island is 1.6 inches, considerably less than for most of the Sahara. Even the immense tundra, covering a tenth of the earth's land surface, waterlogged, seamed with streams and dotted with lakes beyond count, is a near-desert. It only receives between eight and ten inches of precipitation annually.

The explanation to this paradox of a sodden land with an arid climate is permafrost, the layer of permanently frozen ground as much as 1,600 feet deep in some areas of the Arctic. Cement-hard and waterproof, the permafrost keeps all precipitation near the surface, to collect in lakes and bogs, or to run off in rivers and brooks. No moisture can drain away into the ground beyond the reach of the shallow root system of Arctic plants. Without permafrost, the Arctic would be a desert, the largest on earth.

Many Arctic plants are xerophytes, desert-adapted plants with small leathery leaves and stems wrapped in fuzzy fur to prevent moisture loss in the dry Arctic wind. To avoid desiccation, rather than to escape cold, many of the plants bury their winter buds just below the surface of the soil. Arctic plants are adapted to cold to an extent that still mystifies botanists. During a warm spell in early spring, some plants, with more enthusiasm than caution, send the sap coursing through their cells. Buds swell, shoots and twigs throb with juice and life—and suddenly the cold returns and freezes them solid, so they snap at a touch, like fragile icicles. Yet with the next thaw, they continue to expand and live, as if nothing untoward had happened, alternating between life and death, growing when temperatures permit, relapsing into a deathlike, dormant state with the next heavy frost, continuing to live in conditions that would be instantly fatal to southern plants.

As the taiga, the northern forest, reaches its limit, the tree line, the trees become smaller and their roots shallower, expanding only laterally. These trees, bent by winds and snow in many directions, are also tilted hither and yon by upwelling ice, the so-called naled or aufeis. Scientists sometimes refer to these leaning trees as "the drunken forest." They peter out in "the land of the little sticks," as Chipewayan Indians call the very edge of the northern forest, where begins the immensity of the treeless tundra, the true Arctic. Even there trees grow, but except in favoured river valleys, they are small and grovel along the ground: dwarf birches and dwarf willows, creeping juniper and Lapland rhododendron. Their season of growth is short, their season of winter dormancy long, and the thumb-thick stem of a willow may have four hundred or more annual rings.

Spring awakens the plants to life. The snow melts and so does a thin layer of permafrost, providing the plants with moisture and nutrients. This thawed top stratum of earth is known as the "active layer," an ominously apt description in some areas. On slopes and hillsides, the active layer becomes water-saturated in spring and begins to slide downward upon its hard, icy permafrost base. This solifluction, a myriad slow-motion earth avalanches, tears plant roots, buries plants, and scars hills and valleys. Alternate thawing and freezing of water in rock fissures breaks stone. In spring Eskimos rarely set up a tent near the base of a great cliff, because of the threat of rock falls. Immense scree slopes bank most Arctic cliffs, witness to the awesome power of frost and thaw, the great levellers of the Arctic.

In April, a season of frequent gales and sometimes of bitter cold, the first birds arrive from the south. Small snow buntings flit in gay twittering flocks from one bare spot of land to the next, picking up seeds. They nest as far north as there is land, and one snow bunting was seen by crew members of Fridtjof Nansen's ship Fram, drifting through the grim, ice-covered vastness of the Central Polar Basin on May 22, 1895, at eighty-five degrees north, within five degrees of the North Pole. "It fluttered around the ship, twittering, for some time, and then flew off towards the north."

The migration flights of many Arctic birds are marvels of endurance and precision navigation. Pacific golden plovers fly each fall from Alaska to Hawaii and to the tiny island kingdom of Tonga, non-stop flights of two thousand and more miles across the trackless ocean, and these ten-inch birds cover the distance in forty-eight hours.

In recent decades a small passerine bird has invaded the North American Arctic. The wheatear is common in northern Europe, a brownish bird with a flashing white rump and restless, excitable manners. These winged little Vikings spread to Iceland, discovered Greenland in the last century, and are now invading the Canadian Arctic. A few years ago they were still confined to Baffin Island and Labrador. Now they have been seen west of Hudson Bay. But they have never heard of Florida or Mexico, fine places to spend a warm winter. Instead, in fall, guided by the intricate programming of millennial instincts, the wheatears of Arctic Canada fly from Baffin Island to Greenland, from Greenland to Iceland, across the storm-tossed North Atlantic to Britain, and on across France and Spain, to central Africa, as their ancestors have done since the beginnings of wheatear time.

The elegant Arctic terns enjoy more daylight during the year than any other bird. They nest as far north as Ellesmere Island, within a few hundred miles of the North Pole, where the sun shines day and night all summer. In winter they fly far south across the "Roaring Forties" and the "Shrieking Fifties," to the long days of the Antarctic. By the time they return, they have spent nearly seven months on the wing, and have flown about 22,000 miles. One banded Arctic tern is known to have lived twenty-seven years. In its life, this graceful little bird may have flown close to a million miles, shuttling back and forth between the earth's antipodes.

In the Arctic, as everywhere else on earth, green plants are the basis of all life. Their ability to utilize the sun's energy for the process of photosynthesis (the conversion of inorganic substances into sugars and starches) provides food for the entire pyramid of life's myriad forms. The tiny plants of the sea, the phytoplankton, are food for the host of planktonic animals, shrimplike copepods and tiny crustaceans so numerous in early summer that they can colour the sea for miles. These small plant eaters are, in turn, eaten by the predators of the sea, larger crustaceans, fish, and squid, and they are the food of sea mammals. A sixty-ton Greenland whale scoops up and swallows one and a half tons of krill, small crustaceans or snails, each day; and they, to live, eat five and a half trillion sea plants daily. Yet so rich are the seas of Arctic and Antarctic in nutrients, so stupendous is the growth of plants and of the planktonic animals feeding on them, that these frigid polar seas are home to the greatest concentrations of sea mammals on earth. And they, in turn, made it possible for man, the predator at the pinnacle of the food pyramid, to survive in the Arctic.

On land, plant growth in the Arctic is slow and sparse. The annual plant productivity of a given area in terms of weight is only about one percent of that in more favoured regions of the south. Yet the Arctic is vast, and it does have enough plant food for vast numbers of animals. Most numerous of the mammals is the lemming. It feeds on grass and is itself the most important food for a host of predators. Without lemmings, Arctic foxes could not survive in most areas of the Arctic, and in the days before wages and welfare, fox furs were the basis of the Eskimo's barter economy.

In winter, the lemmings, who look like chubby mice with tiny tails and small rounded ears, live in nests of grass underneath the snow. A radiating network of tunnels permits them to reach the nearby vegetation. In spring, even before the snow is gone, the first litter is born, and five or six more litters follow in the course of a good summer. Lemmings in captivity have had as many as sixteen litters in one year. Since the young mate within thirty days of birth, their numbers soon become astronomical.

Lemming populations usually rise and fall in four-year cycles. In peak years, it is difficult to walk across the tundra without stepping on lemmings. They are everywhere, and suddenly whole populations may begin to travel, millions of lemmings—"like the host of God," wrote Pontoppidian, the eighteenth-century bishop of Bergen in Norway—all moving in the same direction. Nothing will stop them or deflect them from their course. They swim across rivers and lakes, and even sea arms, and if these are too wide, most will drown. ". . . yet still we press/Westward, in search, to death, to nothingness," wrote Britain's poet laureate John Masefield of the lemmings' march. These vast, compulsive migrations, often ending in death and disaster, are the basis of the ancient legend of the lemmings' mass suicide.

When lemmings are numerous, Arctic predators prosper. Foxes raise large litters; Arctic owls lay an especially generous clutch of eggs; the mighty polar bear hunts the small rodents; lake trout and char gorge on lemmings and, complained one Labrador visitor, "taste mousey"; and even the meek, herbivorous caribou develops a taste for blood, kills lemmings with its large, splayed hoofs, and eats them.

Few Arctic animals hibernate. The ground is hard and frozen, and winter excessively long. Only the Arctic ground squirrel and its arch-enemy, the Barren Ground grizzly, spend the winter in torpor-like sleep. The ground squirrels, called *siksiks* by the Eskimos, dig their burrows into dry sandy eskers or river banks, which thaw more deeply in summer. They spend summer and fall eating and accumulating fat, and stock their winter burrow with as much as four pounds of provisions. All summer they are busy digging roots, collecting grass and leaves, and nibbling mushrooms. They run back and forth, cheek pouches crammed with food, but when they sense danger and want to avoid detection they crawl flat over the ground, doing "the tundra glide," as one scientist has called it.

In September, having doubled their weight in the brief summer months, the siksiks retire to their burrows, eat most of their stores, and when October's frost seeps through the ground they fall asleep. For six months they rest in a delicate balance between life and death, their body's motor barely idling. The rate of breathing drops from sixty times per minute to once or twice, the body temperature falls from 98° to close to freezing. Despite this rigorous conservation of energy, the ground squirrel's fat reserves are nearly exhausted when it wakes up in April.

When siksiks emerge from their long winter's sleep near an Eskimo camp, they may quickly end up in a pot. For spring to the Eskimos is an ambivalent season. It is a season of promise, of warmth after many months of bitter cold, and of light after winter's depressing darkness.

> There is joy
> In feeling the warmth
> Come to the great world
> And seeing the sun
> Follow its old footprints
> In the summer night.

But spring is also a season when hunting is difficult, travel curtailed, and food can be desperately hard to get. Igloos leak and threaten to collapse; winter's refuse, buried under snow, is now exposed; and most families move to spring camps, setting up their tents on dry gravel ridges. In former days, pokes full of seal oil, collected in winter and weighing two to four hundred pounds each, were stored on islands, safe from marauding foxes, or left under stones on high rock pillars, where not even wolverines or Barren Ground grizzlies could reach them. One such stone pillar in the Bathurst Inlet region served people from several camps, and was probably used for centuries. Even now, after decades of disuse, the twenty-foot-high stack smells faintly of seal oil.

Spring, in the past, was also the season of the Eskimos' dispersal. Families who had clustered together in winter seal-hunting camps now scattered over the immensity of their spring hunting area. They left quietly—as quietly as one can depart with a team of howling, excited huskies. (Eskimos rush out joyfully to meet a visitor. Greetings are elaborate. One is expected to shake hands with everyone, even an infant peeping out of its mother's amautik. But one leaves quietly; and few pay attention. The

Eskimo language has many words of welcome, but none for goodbye.)

In spring, seals enlarge their breathing holes and haul out onto the ice, to bask in the sun. A seal is a fitful sleeper. Every minute or so he wakes up, looks carefully around and, if all seems safe, falls asleep again. In the eastern Arctic, Eskimos approach a seal on the ice hidden behind a portable hunting screen, now made of cloth, formerly of bleached seal or caribou skin. The hunter synchronizes his movements with those of the seal. When the seal awakens, he crouches low behind his white shield. When the seal sleeps, he quickly advances, until he is close enough for a sure shot or, in former days, to throw his harpoon.

In the central Arctic, Eskimos do not use the screen. Instead, they employ a method known to Eskimos from Alaska to Greenland: they approach a seal by pretending to be a seal. The hunter slithers full-length across the snow, while the seal sleeps. When it wakes, the hunter stops, and makes seal-like movements, pretending to scratch himself with a flipper. The seal stares, curious and a bit scared, but if the performance is good, he goes back to sleep reassured that the dark shape on the ice is only a harmless fellow-seal. A skilful hunter needs half an hour to advance within shooting range. But in former days, when he had to approach a seal to within a dozen feet to throw his harpoon, it could take an hour and even two. As long as snow covers the ice, this hunt, though difficult and exhausting, is often successful and not too uncomfortable. But when melt-water covers the ice, and the hunter gets soaking wet, it is a terrible test to his hardiness and endurance.

Early spring, when the snow is still hard, is the Eskimos' favourite season for travelling. The days are long, the cold has lost some of its sting, and since the snow's white surface reflects ninety percent of the sun's heat, it can be very warm during the hours of sunlight. Northern sunlight contains a high percentage of ultraviolet, and these rays can inflame and even burn the eye's conjunctiva. The result is snow blindness, as searingly painful as if sandpaper were rubbed across the eyeballs. Early Eskimos protected themselves against this spring danger with ingenious goggles, carved of wood, bone, or ivory, which admitted light only through a narrow slit in the centre. The intense glare also scorches the faces of Eskimos who, during the long dark days of winter, have paled to their normal skin colour which is not much darker than that of a European. To prevent sunburn and chapped lips and hands, they rub themselves with oil. The best protection, they claim, is the subcutaneous fat of ptarmigan.

To visit and be visited is one of the great joys of Eskimo life. Rasmussen once arrived at an Eskimo camp and, as soon as his igloo was built, a terrible storm broke loose. It was easy to get lost even in the few yards from igloo to igloo, and being lost could mean death. Rasmussen reports, however, that this did not deter the Eskimos from visiting. But each person took his snow knife along as a precaution and, if he did get lost, he "merely [built] himself a little house."

At Bathurst Inlet in 1969, a spring invasion of visitors swelled the population of Ekalun's camp from seventeen to fifty-two. In addition, there were suddenly more than one hundred dogs to feed, yet provisions were at a low ebb. This in no way curbed the Eskimos' happiness at having guests. They vied with each other to provide the most lavish feasts until the last shred of food was gone. Their only regret was that they did not have more to give. "We are not like people in the south who, as they tell me, like to keep things for themselves. What we have, we share," Ekalun said. When the visitors left, the caches were empty. No food remained to be shared, the Eskimos bestirred themselves and, following God's injunction to Noah that "every moving thing that liveth shall be meat for you," shot loons and ducks, plovers and ptarmigan, trapped ground squirrels, and fished for tomcod and whitefish through leads in the ice—and waited, waited endlessly, patiently for the caribou to arrive at their Arctic shores.

To the coastal Eskimos of Greenland, Labrador, Hudson Bay, the Canadian Arctic islands, and Alaska the sea gave life. The land provided only a small portion of their sustenance. The Thule Eskimos of northern Greenland captured with nets some of the millions of dovekies nesting among the scree on mountain slopes, stuffed the birds into sealskin bags, and kept them as a treat for winter. The Eskimos of Hudson Strait visited the soaring cliffs of Cape Wolstenholme and Digges Island (where two million murres nest precariously on narrow ledges) to collect their toll of fat murrelings in fall. The Aivilingmiut—who moved to Southampton Island, after its native Sadlermiut, thought to have been the last descendants of Dorset culture Eskimos, had died of disease—herded flightless, moulting snow geese into elaborate stone pounds and killed them by the hundred. And in fall nearly all the coastal tribes went inland to kill caribou whose fur they needed for winter clothing.

But the bulk of the coastal Eskimos' food came from the Arctic sea: seals and walrus, white whales and narwhal, and occasionally the great Greenland whale. The sea mammals alone enabled them to live in the Arctic, and their hunting methods, their culture, their thoughts, and their legends and lore were moulded by this main preoccupation of their lives: to get food from the sea.

While the coastal Eskimos kept their minds and eyes fixed upon the sea and long ago worshipped Sedna, the sea-goddess, mother of seals and whales, the Caribou Eskimos of the Barrens (and a few inland Eskimo groups in Alaska) looked to the land to give them life. Some groups migrated to the coast to hunt seal in summer; others, like the Harvaqtormiut of the Kazan River region, visited the coast only rarely to obtain seal products by barter. But the sea and its animals were not vital to their existence. For survival they depended nearly entirely upon the caribou. It was uppermost in their thoughts, their legends, and in their entire hunting culture; and in the 1940s and 1950s when caribou failed, fear, famine, and death haunted these specialized hunters of the great Barrens.

The people of Bathurst Inlet and other Eskimo groups along the northern edge of the Arctic mainland combine cultural and hunting elements of both the coastal and the inland Eskimos.

Theirs is a Janus-faced existence. In winter and early spring they look to the sea and its seals to feed them. But once the snow begins to thaw, and birds arrive from the south, the sea loses its lure, and they face south, towards the land, where soon the caribou will come. The talk in camp turns from *netsiak*—the seal—to *tuktu*—the caribou. It may be days yet, even weeks before the first caribou arrive, yet the people talk of tuktu, think of tuktu, even dream of tuktu. Often, in spring, I heard Ekalun mumble in his sleep, next to me on the sleeping platform, and it was "tuktu," always "tuktu," endless herds of caribou migrating through the sleeping mind of the old hunter.

> Glorious it is to see
> The caribou flocking down from the forest
> And beginning
> Their wandering to the north.
> Timidly they watch
> For the pitfalls of man.
> Glorious it is to see
> The great herds from the forests
> Spreading out over the plain of white.
> Glorious to see.

The caribou come still each spring, driven northward by millennial instincts, from the vast forests of the taiga across the immensity of the tundra, a living and life-giving tide, the last great wildlife herds of North America. Yet their numbers are sadly depleted. Once, when the caribou came, an old Eskimo told Rasmussen, "the whole country is alive, and one can see neither the beginning of them nor the end—the whole earth seems to be moving." When J. W. Tyrrell of the Canadian Geological Survey travelled across the Barrens in 1893, then "less . . . known than the remotest regions of 'Darkest Africa,'" he found the caribou beyond count. "They could only be reckoned in acres or square miles."

To the Eskimos of the Barrens and of the Arctic mainland coast, the caribou supplied nearly all their needs. Its meat was their food and that of their dogs. Surplus meat was dried and cached in spring and summer, and cached fresh frozen in fall. Fall furs were tailored into the warmest yet lightest winter clothing existent, and children's suits were made from soft fawn pelts. Dried and shredded sinew provided thread for sewing the clothes. Plaited sinew backed the Eskimos' bows and gave them strength and spring; it served as guy-lines to hold up the caribou-skin tent; and sinew cord was made into fishing lines. Toggles for clothing and dog harnesses were carved of caribou bone. Sharpened splinters of caribou shin bone were set into ice and covered with blood and fat. When a wolf came along and licked the blood, he lacerated his tongue on the frozen-in bone knife, and excited by the taste of fresh blood licked and bled and licked and bled until he died. "The most fiendish trap ever devised," the explorer William H. Gilder called this *alukpa* of the Eskimos.

Caribou antlers were straightened, after being boiled or immersed in hot water, with a big bone or a palmate piece of antler into which a large hole had been worked. (At Bathurst Inlet strong, perforated pieces of moose antler were once used for this purpose.) European archeologists are familiar with this instrument. Rudimentary types are known from the Aurignacian Period thirty thousand years ago, but it was the Magdalenians who, some fifteen thousand years ago, perfected these antler-benders and ornamented them with superb engravings. Under the mistaken impression that these were prehistoric versions of a marshal's bâton, archeologists have called them bâtons de commandement. Any Caribou Eskimo could have identified the implement at first glance. It was nearly identical to the *qatersiorfik* he used to straighten antler pieces which, pegged, glued (with caribou blood), and lashed together, formed his spear shafts, or sections of his dog sled.

Caribou skins, scraped clean of hairs, were cut into thongs, made into bags and containers, and covered the kayaks. The new-born Eskimo baby was wiped clean with a piece of caribou fur, and when an Eskimo died, his shroud was made of caribou skins. Had the world been created with but one animal, the caribou, the Eskimo of the Barrens would have been content.

Since the introduction of firearms, killing caribou has become easy, too easy perhaps, since most authorities consider consistent overhunting the major cause of the caribou's decline from an estimated 3,000,000 in the last century to a low of 200,000 by 1960. (Since reaching this nadir, the caribou of the Canadian tundra-taiga have increased again to at least 300,000.) But before they had guns, caribou-hunting Eskimos had to rely on simple weapons, great ingenuity, infinite patience and hardiness, and a superb knowledge of caribou behaviour to kill the one to two hundred animals each family and its dog needed per year in order to survive.

Although some caribou remained on the Barrens and near the Arctic coast all winter, few were hunted. To approach the shy animals across the hard, creaking winter snow to within bow-and-arrow range of twenty paces was nearly impossible. Some caribou were trapped and killed in pitfalls dug into snow drifts. In spring, Eskimos waited in circular stone ambushes, built in the path of main migration routes, for caribou to approach. Often they huddled in this confined space for days, waiting for a caribou to come close enough for a shot.

> Here I stand
> Surrounded with great joy
> For a caribou bull with high antlers
> Recklessly exposed his flanks to me.
> Oh, how I had to crouch
> In my hide.

Caribou are curious and shortsighted, and Eskimo hunting strategems took advantage of both these weaknesses. Two men walked past a herd. As they passed a boulder one hid behind, the other continued, waving, perhaps, a piece of white caribou belly skin to attract the curious animals. They followed him at a safe distance—and were shot by the hidden hunter.

Walking together—one man with hands raised to imitate antlers, the second bent forward—two men, whose joint silhouette then vaguely resembled that of a caribou, could sometimes come close enough to the myopic animals for a shot. And, semi-legendary, there were Eskimos who could run *qahapqanguartalerpai*—at such a speed that one scarcely touches the ground—and who simply outran the caribou and killed them with knives or spears. But that, of course, was *taitsumani*—long, long ago!

Most caribou were killed in fall from kayaks at favourite crossing places in lakes or rivers, or in spring and summer in elaborate ambushes one still finds at strategic locations in the Barrens and near the Arctic coast. Here the Eskimos built alignments of *inukshuks* (literally "something acting in the capacity of a man"). These stone pillars resembled people from a distance, and served to frighten caribou in the direction of the *tallo*, the shooting pits, where hunters waited for them. Women and children, hidden behind ridges and boulders supplemented the line of inukshuks and, at a signal, rose and screamed ("hoo-hoo-hoo they yelled, just like wolves," Ekalun recalled), and waved skins to stampede the caribou towards the hidden hunters, who shot them with arrows and even speared them. To succeed, this hunt had to be carried out with military precision. Dr. W. E. Taylor of the National Museum of Canada has pointed out that 'the enfiladed arrangement of the shooting pits to give support in depth and to focus killing power on a concentrated target might have been taken from a recent military manual." Many of these ambuscades were used for centuries. Indeed some Eskimo groups credit the long-extinct, semi-mythical Tunit (the Dorset culture people) with having invented and constructed the most elaborate of the inukshuk-flanked ambushes.

Before the advent of white men and their guns, the Eskimos lived in balance with nature or, as Dr. Ian McTaggart Cowan has put it, "The native people were a dynamic element in the balanced ecosystem." While this may sound very commendable, in practice it simply meant that the Eskimos periodically starved to death so that their numbers never increased to the point where they could have seriously decimated those game animals upon which they depended for food. Rasmussen's diligent inquiries have shown that even the best Netsilik hunters using the primitive weapons of former times managed only to kill seventy to eighty caribou each year, plus some thirty seals in winter and spring. They were not conservationists at heart. They killed as much as they could and that, usually, was barely enough for subsistence. For many groups, it was a life of alternating feast and famine and, in some years—the bad years—feasts were short and famines fatally long.

Like their animal predator-competitors, the wolf and the polar bear, the Eskimos could and, at least in camps, still can eat incredible quantities of food when it is available. A polar bear can stuff himself with 150 pounds of blubber at a sitting. A wolf can gulp down twenty pounds of caribou meat, a fourth of his own weight. And a hungry Eskimo can eat ten pounds of caribou meat and be ready for the next meal a few hours later. Among the Netsilingmiut, Rasmussen records, it is a common saying that for a hungry man two fat raw char represent a meal. That is about twelve pounds of fish. While travelling with George Hakungak of Bathurst Inlet on a two-week spring caribou hunt, we (four adults and nine dogs) ate a caribou a day, and when the hunting was good and we were really hungry, we ate nearly two. At that rate even the meat piles from a successful spring hunt quickly disappear.

Many explorers and scientists have accused the Eskimos of living only for the present with no thought for the future. The famous anthropologist Birket-Smith called the Caribou Eskimos "skilful hunters, but very improvident." Undoubtedly they were both, though some allowance must be made for the hazards of the hunt and the difficulty in laying up stores for lean months ahead. When it was possible, most Eskimos were provident. Seal oil in pokes made of whole sealskins was stored in early spring for the difficult days of late fall when seal would be hard to hunt and oil for food and lamps impossible to obtain. "A single family's store of oil for the fall will run from nine hundred to two thousand pounds," Stefansson observed. In spring and summer caribou meat was dried and this *mipku* cached for hungry days. During peak hunting seasons, coastal Eskimos sometimes amassed great stores of seal and walrus meat and buried it under piles of stones to protect it—not always successfully—from marauding polar bears; and during the fall fishing season, char were split and dried and stored away for winter.

But sometimes, there is little to save. When I left Bathurst Inlet in late fall, caribou hunting was nearly finished, yet there was only enough meat to last our camp a few weeks. Fishing had been poor. In spring, Hakungak wrote: "We never go for trapping this winter because too much blowing and sometime no food for the dogs. Sometime when clear weather we go out to look for agloos but our dogs are so weak we never find agloos. We now using only six puppys and two left old ones. . . . No caribou this winter." Characteristically, the letter ends, "People here at Bathurst Inlet doing very fine."

With the advent of spring, the worst is over. While the coming of winter and darkness brings gloom to the land and the Eskimo mind—a despondency they tried to shake off by making this their most festive season with songs and games and dances—spring brings hope and life and light. Already in March, ravens circle and swoop high in the sky in the intricate gyrations of their nuptial flights, and their resonant croaks echo from the cliffs where they will soon build their nests, a month earlier than any other bird in the Arctic.

In April the sun becomes intense, its heat reflected off the glittering snow. Snow evaporates from ridges and tussocks, only to be replaced by blinding spring blizzards. But it is warmer now. The sled dogs, who in winter curl into tight balls, noses tucked under bushy tails, now loll leisurely upon the snow.

In May the land begins to change. At noon on sunny days, evaporation vapour dances and shimmers above the ground and patches of snow-free ground become larger. Arctic hares, still immaculately white in early May, flit nervously across the bare ground, as if aware how conspicuous they suddenly are against a backdrop of dark earth. The female ptarmigan begins to moult, brown feathers replace the white winter plumage, but the cock still remains pure white, except for his "rose," the serrated wattle above each eye, now glowing vermilion in the excitement of spring and mating.

Anything dark lying upon snow or ice absorbs the sun's warming rays; and pebbles, twigs, old leaves, seeds, and little piles of ptarmigan droppings burn holes through ice and snow. A pebble the size of a marble can create a hole in solid ice nearly a foot across and two to three feet deep.

In late May the snow becomes soft, mushy, and waterlogged. Travel overland is difficult and Eskimos sledge at night, when frost hardens the snow. The mud covering of the runners melts and falls off. In camp, the women are busy making waterproof sealskin boots for their families, boots whose double-crimped seams are ingeniously sewn with the "blind stitch" technique in which the needle never completely pierces the skin. (Unlike women in most other lands, Eskimo women sew from right to left, rather than from left to right.) In the past, when good clothing was vital to a hunter's success and survival, women were valued at least as much for their skill with the needle as for their looks. In the Eskimo legend, Navaranaq, a girl who betrays her people to the Indians, later pleads with her countrymen for her life and, stressing her assets, points out that she is "a clever seamstress and good to lie with."

For months, the Eskimos have been as sedentary as is possible for an essentially nomadic people. Now, of course, they trap in winter and make extensive journeys, but in the past they moved little during the winter months. But in spring, there is change and restlessness in the air. Winter clothing is dried in the sun, packed, and cached. Winter weapons are stored away. One family leaves to fish at a distant lake. Another travels inland to intercept the long-awaited caribou. The camp cohesion of winter disintegrates, and the group divides into its basic units: one or two families who wander together during late spring, summer, and fall, and coalesce briefly with other families at favourite fishing rivers or in areas where caribou are usually numerous, and then divide again and wander on, each family following its own mood and its own hopes for a successful summer hunt. Before Europeans came to the Arctic, the Eskimo was "to a degree that we today can hardly comprehend . . . free and independent, master of his own fate," wrote the anthropologist Diamond Jenness. And Stefansson, who also lived among Eskimos who had never before seen a white man echoes this: "The Eskimo individually behaves like a sovereign state. The laws of others do not bind him, and he makes new laws for himself whenever he likes."

Though camps are more stable and permanent now than they used to be, the urge to move, to see, to travel, and to roam still grips the Eskimos in spring. Within one week in May, our camp at Bathurst Inlet shrunk from seven families to two. Some returned after a week or so, others we did not see again till late in fall.

There is joy
In feeling the warmth
Come to the great world.

In the blue-grey light of a spring night, an Eskimo pulls a shot wolf back to camp.

Helped by his wife, the hunter skins the wolf.

Like washing on the line, wolf skins hang at camp to dry in the spring sun.

Wet snow softens the dogs' pads in spring, and sharp ice cuts their paws. Eskimos put booties (now made of canvas or duck, formerly of skin) on their dogs for spring travel. Most dogs hate the booties, but know from experience that they will be punished if they chew them off.

In spring, Eskimos move their camps to dry, sheltered ridges. Winter clothes are dried and cached. Seal-hunting gear is stowed away. The move to the spring camps is a festive occasion. In the seasonal migrations of the Eskimos, it marks the end of winter.

As the ice begins to shift in the spring, wide leads open near the shore. Dogs harnessed to a sled are reluctant to cross them. But occasionally one can entice them across by jumping over the lead with them. Jumping leads near camp in spring is one of the Eskimo children's favourite pastimes.

Nearly invisible in their white winter camouflage, white Arctic hares nibble the sere grass among rocks on a mountain slope. These large hares can weigh up to twelve pounds. In winter their fur is pure white, only the tips of their ears are black.

Overleaf: As soon as the snow begins to melt in spring, the female ptarmigan changes into camouflage plumage. The cock remains white for another month and, usually perched on a knoll or boulder in the vicinity of the nest, is a tempting target for predators, while the camouflaged hen broods her eggs in peace.

The large glaucous gulls, pure white with a pale-grey mantle, arrive in the Arctic early in spring.

As leads open in the ice, Eskimos set nets to catch whitefish.

Food is short in camp, and an Eskimo woman sets traps to catch Arctic ground squirrels.

The land looks empty, but the Eskimo woman knows where the ground squirrel colonies are.

Stone pillars, called inukshuks by Eskimos, roughly man-shaped in silhouette, were erected long ago to scare the migrating caribou towards places where Eskimo hunters lay in ambush.

Searching the land for caribou, an old Eskimo hunter scans the valley and the sea shore below a ridge. Binoculars and guns have made hunting easier, but game is scarcer now than it was in former days. Spring caribou are lean, but once seal hunting has ceased, the Eskimos impatiently await their arrival in the north.

Having run down and shot a wounded caribou, a hunter awaits the arrival of the dog sled.

The men hunt, the women cut up the meat in slabs and hang it up to dry.

SUMMER

Summer in the Arctic is short. While plants and animals in the south have months to reproduce their kind, life's cycle in the north is compressed within a few brief weeks. Frost often lingers until late June and may return in the middle of August. The climate is arid, the soil usually acid, poorly drained, and badly aerated. Bacterial decay is slow, and the earth, in consequence, deficient in nitrogen and other nutrients. Despite these harsh and hostile conditions, the Arctic is home to some nine hundred flowering plants, two thousand species of lichen and five hundred of mosses. Even on icy Pearyland, desert-dry and forbiddingly rugged, within five hundred miles of the North Pole, ninety species of flowers grow.

To endure and prosper in such an inclement land, plants have developed many adaptive features to ensure survival. Scientists had long been intrigued by the fact that many Arctic plants achieve the seemingly impossible: to grow at temperatures too low for photosynthesis. Such plants usually bunch in dense clusters, and closer investigation reveals that within this clump of dark-coloured vegetation, absorbing and retaining the sun's warming rays, the temperature can be from twenty to thirty degrees higher than the surrounding air temperature. Thanks to this microclimate, the season of growth for such plants is appreciably lengthened.

Only one percent of all Arctic plants are annuals, completing their life's cycle within one season. The perennials, which may take two or even as many as ten years from germination to flowering, play it slow but safe. A bad season may retard their growth, it will not wipe them out. Some Arctic plants dispense with seeds altogether and propagate their species purely vegetatively. They send out runners and turions, subterranean shoots, to start new plants, or they grow bulbils, aerial buds that often emerge in leaf axils and drop from the mother plant to form plants of their own. And many plants, hedging their bets in the risky lottery of Arctic life, reproduce both vegetatively and through seeds.

Plants growing on hills and ridges, swept nearly bare of snow in winter, are exposed to extreme cold, to snow and sand abrasion and to the desiccating winds of winter. But they are the first to gain warmth from the spring sun, and it is here that one finds the first flowers, gay little rosettes of purple saxifrage. In the valleys and in the lee of hills and mountains, plants lie cosily covered by winter's thick blanket of snow. Snow is an excellent insulator, and in winter the temperature below two feet of snow may be fifty or sixty degrees higher than the air temperature. But in early summer, while flowers already bloom on the hills, the "snow-bed" plants are still buried beneath slowly melting drifts, and when they finally emerge their season of growth is extremely short.

To collect moisture and prevent evaporation, the moss campion, growing on sandy ridges and eskers, forms thick, petal-spangled cushions. Dwarf willows and dwarf birches often grow next to big boulders, and their branches embrace the south sides, tentacle-like, to absorb warmth from the sun-heated stone. On the immense Arctic meadows, sedges and grasses, pushed up by frost heaving, cling together in dense mop-headed tussocks which botanists, a bit cavalierly, call *têtes de femme*.

Whatever else they lack, Arctic plants have an abundance of daylight during their growing season. The "long-day" plants of the north, transplanted to the more genial south, wither and die. Inversely, "short-day" plants of southern regions do not necessarily prosper in the north's continuous daylight, even in greenhouses, and when they do, they are likely to behave quite erratically. Cucumbers grown in steamheated, well-watered greenhouses in the Russian coal-mining towns of Spitsbergen on rich earth and under continuous sunlight develop with the breath-taking speed of science-fiction plants and, unless rigorously trimmed, produce a jungle-like growth of shoots and leaves, but no fruit whatever.

Death and decay are essential links in the chain of life. In death and through decomposition, plants and animals return to the earth and sea those minerals essential to the life of future generations. This eternal recycling of life's basic components also takes place in the Arctic, but cold slows both growth and decay. The wooden slabs marking the graves of members of the Franklin expedition on Beechey Island are as solid today as when they were erected more than a century ago. Some tree trunks from Siberia, washed ashore by Arctic currents on Spitsbergen and buried under gravel, were discovered to be thousands of years old. For more than a century Netsilik Eskimos travelled to Victoria Harbour on Boothia Peninsula where Sir John Ross had left a profusion of material and provisions which did not decay. *Qilanartut*, the Eskimos called the place, "the beach of joyful hopes." A few mammoths, buried in Siberia's permafrost, were well enough preserved to allow Russian scientists the rare treat of eating 25,000-year-old mammoth steaks. The stomach contents of some of these prehistoric, woolly elephants of taiga and tundra had not decomposed in 250 centuries, and showed botanists that the same plants that once sustained the mammoth now feed muskox, hare, and caribou.

In summer, Arctic plants seem to grow and mature with amazing rapidity. Within days, the somber, brown-grey tundra of spring is carpeted for miles with dainty flowers. The sight of "the Barrens bursting into bloom" never fails to amaze visitors, yet the development is not quite as abrupt as it may seem. The buds actually began to form in the fall. Then they lay dormant during winter, only to continue development the moment weather in spring permits. Some plants, like the Arctic poppy, need less than a month from beginning of growth to the production of ripe seeds.

Although growth seems so rapid in summer, the cumulative annual growth and weight increase of Arctic plants is extremely low, only about one percent of that in southern regions. McClintock, searching for the missing Franklin expedition on Melville Island in 1853, was amazed to see that cart tracks left in 1820 by Sir Edward Parry's expedition had hardly a trace of moss on them and even now, one hundred and fifty years later, these tracks are clearly visible. On July 1, 1767, the explorer Samuel Hearne scraped his name into a sloping rock wall near the mouth of the Churchill River. After two centuries, no trace of lichen obscures his florid signature. And, it is safe to say, ten generations hence people will be able to see, and perhaps curse, the scars and gashes left now by the giant-tracked vehicles that lumber across the Arctic land and churn up its thin and fragile plant cover in the frantic search for oil and minerals.

Since Arctic soil is nutrient-poor, anything that will provide nitrates or phosphates stimulates a rich growth. Like many-coloured jewels, various species of lichen encrust pieces of bone and antler. Where great whales have been killed long ago, dense clusters of flowers grow around their slowly decomposing bones. Boulders in the Barrens, favourite perches of owls and hawks, are streaked in brilliant orange by the nitrophilous lichen Caloplaca elegans. The dens of wolves, foxes, and ground squirrels can be seen from afar (and are easily spotted in aerial surveys) as oases of rich-green vegetation in drabber surroundings. A few plants, such as the elegant Pallas' wallflower, make a career of being coprophilous or dung-loving, and are found mainly near animal burrows or bird colonies. Their seeds stick, burr-like, to animals' fur and are thus transported to new locations. And wherever Eskimos have lived for any length of time, recently or five centuries ago, luxuriant plant growth bears testimony to their existence. Unlike the white man's unassimilable metal-plastic-glass garbage, the organic waste Eskimos left nature could convert again into life's primary building blocks.

For Arctic animals, too, there is a tremendous urgency to breed, to grow, and to mature within summer's brief span. In April, when the raven nests it is so cold that were the female to leave the nest for only a short time, her eggs would freeze solid. Muskox calves, wrapped in thick wool and incredibly hardy, are born in April and May, sometimes at temperatures of −30°F.

Many Arctic animals change from winter white into summer camouflage. Arctic foxes, looking puny in their short-haired, brindled summer pelts, stalk lemmings on the tundra meadows. The Arctic hare in brown-grey fur blends completely with its surroundings, but in the high Arctic where the snow-free season is exceedingly short, the hares remain white even in summer. While the female ptarmigan, fully moulted into mottled grey-brown-black summer plumage, sits quietly and nearly invisible on her eggs, the cock, extremely conspicuous in white feathers, perches on a nearby boulder or hummock. Nature, it seems, has assigned the cock a sacrificial role. Studies in Alaska have shown that predators in summer kill mainly male ptarmigan, while the hidden females safely raise the next generation.

Last of all the birds to arrive in the Arctic, and first to leave, are the phalaropes, robin-sized birds with peculiar habits. Although they belong to the waders, they spend most of their life far out at sea. Their dense plumage holds a cushion of air, and phalaropes bob cork-like across the waves. They arrive in late June or early July in the Arctic, pirouette buoyantly on ice-free ponds, and dab for aquatic insects and crustaceans in the roiled water with sewing-machine rapidity. The female is brightly coloured in russets and reds, the male wears more modest attire. The female does the courting, the male builds the nest. The female lays the eggs, but the male broods them and mothers the chicks. In early August, most adults leave the Arctic again and, about two weeks later, some can be seen riding the waves off Chile and Argentina. Some phalarope males and the chicks follow in the fall.

In their lovely creation legends, the Eskimos tell of the boy who lived alone with his grandmother. Once, in his kayak, he was caught by an off-shore storm. For three days and three nights he paddled frantically, turning this way and that. Blood burst from his face and streaked his clothes, and gradually he became transformed into a phalarope. His grandmother, who, crying and calling, ran along the shore until her sealskin boots were worn and splayed, was turned into the web-footed loon, whose melancholy cry still quavers across the waters.

In many Eskimo dialects July is known as "mosquito month." On a calm, warm day, myriad mosquitoes surround every living being like clouds of smoke, driving man and beast frantic. Caribou flee to wind-swept hills to escape these winged tormentors. Sled dogs dig holes into the ground and curl tightly into them to find some protection. Eskimos used to wear mosquito nets made from the long guard hairs of muskoxen; they burnt smoldering dryas leaves in smudge pots in their tents and, outside, beat their faces with loonskin swatters with metronome regularity.

On the whole, though, Eskimos accept the summer mosquito plague with the same equanimity with which they endure winter's cold. It is part of life and nature and fate, and summer, essentially, is the season they like best.

Rasmussen, spending some time at a Netsilingmiut summer fishing camp, where the people awaited the char, wrote: "Never in my life have I seen such frolicsome and happy people, so gaily starving, so cheerfully freezing in miserable, ragged clothes." The Eskimos played and danced and joked endlessly, and when Rasmussen seemed amazed, an old man told him: "In summer people must flourish in exactly the same manner as the soil they live on."

In late June and early July, ice still covers most bays and inlets, deep blue where the snow has melted, flooded with water and rent by fissures and leads. Sharp ice crystals cut the sled dogs' paws, and Eskimos make them booties of sealskin or, now, of duck or canvas. Once the ice has been broken and dispersed by the wind, the coastal Eskimos in the past commenced their summer kayak hunting. In the eastern and western Arctic the Eskimos formerly used two types of skin-boats: the large open umiak and the sleek covered kayak. The umiak had once probably been primarily a whaling boat, but when whale hunting ceased it became the "women's boat," in which women and children migrated from one hunting area to another. Now the umiak has died out, except at the two extremes of its former range. It is still used by Eskimos of Bering Strait and, nearly six thousand miles away, by the people of Greenland's east coast.

The kayak, one of the most efficient and certainly one of the most beautiful hunting boats ever designed by man, is also disappearing. Now it is only used by a few Eskimos on the Belcher Islands and in some places in northern Greenland and in Alaska. But long ago, it was the main hunting craft of all Eskimos, from Siberia to East Greenland, with one exception. The Polar Eskimos of the Thule and Inglefield Bay region of northwestern Greenland, where the open-water season only lasts a few weeks and driftwood is extremely scarce, had been isolated from all other Eskimos for centuries, so long they had come to think of themselves as the only people on earth. They had also forgotten how to build kayaks. Only the name remained, designating a mythical craft. Then, in 1864, a small group of people from Baffin Island made the most amazing Eskimo migration of modern times: from the Admiralty Inlet area to Thule. They were guided by the greatest shaman of their time, Kritlaq, who the Eskimos aver led his people, nearly as God once had led His children out of bondage in Egypt, driving ahead of them through the polar night with fire and flames shooting from his head. It was these Baffin Island Eskimos who again taught the people closest to the Pole the ancient art of kayak building and kayak hunting.

In the eastern and western Arctic, the kayak was the Eskimos' summer hunting boat and occasionally they also used it for long travels. An Aleut paddled his *baidarka* (Aleutian kayak) 130 miles in thirty hours, but died of a lung hemorrhage. In 1948, four men from the Belcher Islands paddled their kayaks to Richmond Gulf on the east coast of Hudson Bay, about two hundred miles away. It took them four days and three nights.

The Eskimos of the central Arctic did not know the umiak, and used kayaks only for inland travel, to cross rivers and lakes and, above all, to spear caribou at crossing places. Their kayaks, since they had to be carried great distances, were extremely light. While the strong but bulky Baffin Island and Labrador type kayaks can weigh a hundred pounds and more, and even the elegantly streamlined Greenland kayaks weigh about seventy-five pounds, the caribou-skin covered, dwarf-willow frame kayak of the Bathurst Inlet region weighs barely twenty-five pounds. Round-bottomed and light, it is an extremely cranky craft. When one of Rasmussen's Eskimo companions, an expert kayakman from Greenland, tried to paddle one, he promptly capsized.

The central Eskimos were, of course, expert in using these tippy boats. Often they had many, leaving them cached at strategic crossing points. If, on their long inland treks in search of caribou, they had to cross a river and had no kayak along, and none was cached nearby, they made a big parcel of their caribou-skin tent and clothes and used this as a raft.

In the past, Eskimos were truly a travelling people. People from Cumberland Sound on Baffin Island sledged occasionally to Igloolik in northwestern Foxe Basin to trade. Eskimos from Victoria Island travelled nearly a thousand miles to fetch wood in the Thelon River region, and people from the Ungava coast walked across northern Labrador to trade, a two-month return trip on foot in summer, each man carrying close to a hundred pounds.

Sketch maps drawn for the explorer Charles Francis Hall by an Aivilik Eskimo revealed the man was familiar with the coast line from the Churchill River to Lancaster Strait, a direct distance of more than one thousand miles.

In the 1890s, when hunting failed, some forty Eskimos, men, women, and children from the Povungnituk region of eastern Hudson Bay, set out in one umiak to search for game. After sailing for two months, they finally reached the Ottawa Islands more than one hundred miles off the coast. There they lived for many years before resuming their wanderings.

Atangala, an Eskimo of the western Hudson Bay region, served the British traveller David T. Hanbury as guide on his famous trip from Chesterfield Inlet to Coppermine. On the way back, Atangala heard there were white men on King William Island, made a detour of a few hundred miles, and visited Roald Amundsen, then halfway through the Northwest Passage he would eventually conquer. Atangala picked up the white men's mail, sledged to Roe's Welcome Sound, Hudson Bay, to deliver it to whalers and a Canadian government ship spending the winter there. He then picked up mail from them for Amundsen and sledged all the way back to King William Island! He had left with Hanbury in 1902 and he did not return home until 1905.

Ekalun of Bathurst Inlet said his people regularly obtained needles, files, and knives long before white men came to their area, in barter from Eskimos of the Hudson Bay region, who were in contact with whalers. Stefansson has estimated that trade articles, particularly the highly prized jade found only in Alaska, could pass within two and a half years from Bering Strait to Hudson Bay. And Alaskan Eskimos, before the coming of whites, were already familiar with tobacco and pipe. These products of America, having made in trade the tour of the world, reached Alaska from Siberia.

The birthplaces of Ekalun's children reflect the extent of their parents' travels in former days. The oldest son was born near the coast of Coronation Gulf; a daughter near Back River, more than four hundred miles away; another son not far from Contwoyto Lake, three hundred miles further west. When George Hakungak, Ekalun's son, got married, he and his wife Jessie took off on a three-month honeymoon walk, with two pack dogs, a tent, some clothes, a gun and ammunition, a net, a pot, and a few dishes. Food they did not take along. "That we got from the land and the rivers," George explained. One day, at our camp at Bathurst Inlet, two teenage boys arrived on foot. They had been walking for two weeks. When I asked them why they had come, they said: "We felt like visiting."

In the past Eskimos travelled rarely, if ever, for travel's sake. Their endless wanderings were forced upon them by the need to obtain raw materials, to pursue game, to barter and to visit. But although travelling was a necessity, they also liked it, they enjoyed the space, and the freedom and the movement. The Canadian writer Doug Wilkinson, who lived for a year with an Eskimo family in the Pond Inlet area, once told his host about New York. It gave the Eskimo nightmares: "I see people stacked up one atop the other . . . [and] I lie there thinking of what life must be like for all those poor people in New York. . . . I like the sky over my head and the feel of the snow-covered ice beneath my feet. I like to look about and feel myself free."

The summer migrations were not easy. Everything the family needed had to be carried on the people's backs, and the loads were bulky and heavy. The man carried the caribou-skin tent and his weapons, his wife the youngest infant, the stone cooking pot, chunks of pyrite to make fire, tinder, and other household essentials. The children carried whatever their strength permitted, and the dogs were loaded down with packs weighing from forty to fifty pounds. In the days before guns made hunting relatively easy, and when game was scarce, the often gay and happy summer trek could turn into a grim march of the doomed.

> Hungry and starving
> I staggered over the land
> For ever stumbling forward.
>
> I did so wish to see
> Swimming caribou or fish in a lake.
> That joy was my only wish.

To the old, in particular, the long migrations of summer brought severe suffering, trying desperately to keep up with the fast pace of the younger people. When their strength and stamina failed, they were sometimes abandoned with some provisions near a fish-rich river, to fend for themselves as best they could. An old Eskimo woman once asked Rasmussen for the gift of a needle and a thimble and, being poor, said: "I can only repay you with a wish. And that is: May you live long! But if I were to add another wish to these words, a wish that comes from the experience that my age gives me, it is this: May you never be as old as I am!"

Eskimos did not really know how old they were. Even Ekalun was not sure. "We did not count years when I was young," he said. Time is a vague and unimportant concept, and the white man's preoccupation with exact time and exact distances mystifies and annoys the Eskimo mind. Ekalun had two watches and one alarm clock and set them conscientiously each day by the radio. But this careful attention to time existed on a separate plane from his real life, as an abstract entity, and it in no way influenced his daily activities which were regulated not by time but by necessity and by his moods. He slept when he liked, worked when he liked, hunted when he liked. Mood, weather, and need were the determinatives of his life, the time that his watches showed had little relevance. The watches kept time for their own sake, not for his.

When the anthropologist Diamond Jenness visited Eskimos on Victoria Island who had had no contact with whites, he found they "knew nothing of days or weeks; they kept no reckoning even of months, only of the changing seasons as they affected their food supply." Nor could they count very far. "Their language contained no word for any number beyond six," and most of the people he met only got as far as three or, at best, four. Even now large numbers are as difficult to grasp for older Eskimos, as are concepts like light-years and other outer-space statistics for most of us. Ekalun once asked me how many

people live in Montreal and when told "two million," looked puzzled and asked: "How many people is that?" I tried to explain, but did not succeed. How does one explain two million people to a man who has never seen more than four hundred?

But now all Eskimos can count and they do so in six languages. Up to ten, most count in Eskimo. Beyond that, they use Russian in Siberia, Danish in most of Greenland, English in Alaska and most of Arctic Canada, French in a few Arctic Quebec settlements, and German along the Labrador coast where the Moravian missionaries, for nearly two centuries, were usually Germans. (The Labrador Eskimos also use German names for days: Montagami, Dienstagami, Mitwogami, etc.)

Time and numbers meant little to the Eskimos of the past. Their main concern was food, how and where to obtain it, and, above all, to obtain it in quantities sufficient for themselves and their dogs. The coastal as well as the inland Eskimos concentrated their hunting efforts on the largest game available. Everything remotely edible, from lemmings to larks, was eaten in times of dearth, but seals, walrus, and caribou were the mainstay of Eskimo life. Where birds were numerous, they were hunted in summer with the *nui*, the multi-pronged bird dart, usually propelled with a throwing board, or spear thrower, an instrument man had already invented tens of thousands of years ago in Upper Palaeolithic time. Using the principle of the lever, it multiplies the force of an arm's thrust and can propel a seal harpoon or a bird dart for a great distance at high speed. The central Eskimos and those of Alaska also used the bola to capture birds. The bola consisted of stone or ivory balls tied together with long thongs and hurled into a flight of birds. *Quilamitautit*—"those [stones] with which one gets something entangled," the Eskimos called the bola. Strangely enough, this instrument was only used at the two extremes of the American continents: in the Arctic by the Eskimos to catch birds and, some eight thousand miles further south, by the Indians of Patagonia, and now by gauchos, to capture rheas and guanacos.

Most bird hunting, though, the Eskimos left to the children. Once camp had been set up in a likely hunting area, the men went off to hunt caribou, the women collected resinous heather, the favourite summer fuel, or fished for trout and char in nearby lakes, and the children stalked waders and ptarmigan and ducks, shooting at the birds with blunt-tipped arrows to stun them. As families migrated from area to area, surplus food, unneeded tools and clothes, kayaks, sleds, and all sorts of weapons and household articles were cached, to be picked up at the end of the season, perhaps in winter by dog sled, or possibly only during the next year's migration. As a result, the belongings of a family might be scattered over a tremendous area, but unless wolverines or bears had broken into their caches, they could be certain of finding their food and goods intact. Theft among the Eskimos was extremely rare—"among us it is only the dogs that steal," a Chantrey Inlet Eskimo told Rasmussen. A person close to starvation was considered justified in emptying another man's food cache, and in some areas any food cached longer than a year was considered public property. Weapons, tools, clothes, and dogs were strictly private property. They could be borrowed from neighbours and were usually carefully treated. But if an Eskimo accidentally damaged another's equipment, he showed little remorse, especially if the owner was angry, because, they explain, "it is sufficient for one person to feel annoyed."

In these dying days of Eskimo culture and custom, the one trait least changed is the Eskimos' attitude to children, not only in camps, where their ancient way of life has not yet altogether vanished, but even in the European-culture-dominated settlements. Children are born with a minimum of fuss, and raised with a lot of love and little discipline. Eskimo women, Freuchen reported, used to refer to giving birth as a mere "inconvenience." Mary, Ekalun's daughter, served us a copious supper at 1 a.m. when the men of the camp returned late from a long seal hunt; bore a daughter at 2 a.m. and prepared breakfast for all twenty-one people in camp at 7 a.m. Navarana, Freuchen's Eskimo wife, gave birth to a son in the morning and in the evening attended the party Knud Rasmussen gave to celebrate the event and "didn't stop dancing till very late."

The famous anthropologist Franz Boas noted on Baffin Island that Eskimo parents "are very fond of their children and treat them kindly. They are never beaten and rarely scolded, and in turn they are very dutiful, obeying the wishes of their parents and taking care of them in their old age." During the five years I have spent in the Arctic, I have only once seen an Eskimo strike a child. One Eskimo, shocked at the extent to which his people have changed in the large settlement of Frobisher Bay, listed at the top of their newly acquired, non-Eskimo characteristics, "they beat their children."

Stefansson believed the *laissez-faire* attitude of Eskimos towards children to be rooted in their religious beliefs. When a person died, the Eskimos formerly thought his soul (or at least one of his souls; some Eskimo groups believed people had multiple souls) hovered in a rather poorly defined limbo. After a child had been born to relatives of the dead person, his name was given to the infant. His soul then entered into the child and guided it safely through its formative years. To punish the child would have been an insult to its guardian spirit and consequently children were never beaten and rarely rebuked.

Eskimos love children, and men and women never weary of playing with a baby or a young child and are delighted by its antics. Their patience with small children seems inexhaustible, and they have a deep, strong love for all children. The idea of a child's being "illegitimate" and unwanted, just because it was born to an unmarried woman, was until recently foreign to the Eskimo mind. The girl could keep the child and, especially if it was a boy, it was a distinct asset to her future marital prospects and would be considered by her husband as his own child. Or she could give the child up for adoption. This never presented a problem (except, perhaps, in former days with girl children) because childless couples or couples with few children were (and still are) always eager to adopt a child. The adopted child is considered to be the child of its adopted parents and is brought up exactly as a couple's own children. Ekalun, for instance, adopted one of his grandsons, who was from then on referred to by his real father as "my brother."

In the far-off days of blood-feuds (and at the time when, because of girl infanticides, there was a shortage of women) when one man murdered another to obtain his wife, he nearly invariably raised with the greatest love the dead man's sons, fully aware that once they had grown to manhood they were bound by the rules of revenge to kill him.

Discipline-conscious European explorers, visitors, and, later, educators were often mystified by the fact that, although Eskimo children were never disciplined and nearly always allowed to do as they pleased, they were nevertheless amazingly well behaved. Eskimo education is largely based upon the precept that a child, given its own way, will learn by practical experience what is good and what is bad and, without much coercion, will choose the good. As a result Eskimo children are usually very independent and full of self-confidence. In summer, especially they play half the night (it would never occur to the adults to send them to bed at a specific time), sleep when they are tired, eat when they are hungry. And just as adults of a group in former days were kept in line through the rule of public opinion, and transgressions were curbed with cutting lampoon songs, so are the young controlled by the occasional dart of ridicule.

The biologist Sally Carrighar was told by an Alaskan Eskimo, "Eskimo parents do not approve of striking a child, because then the child will feel ugly. He will want to strike someone himself....We were encouraged to be good–not scolded. We could feel we were being loved, and that made us love right back." Explaining to Miss Carrighar how she brought up her children, an Eskimo woman said, "We talk [to the children] every day about being good....Children know [what is good]. ...Nobody has to tell them. They just know what goodness is. When they are born they know. We keep reminding them when they forget."

The result of such gentle, unobtrusive parental guidance is that nearly every visitor to the north has marvelled how gay and well behaved Eskimo children are. "We never saw a child struck or punished, and a more obedient and better lot of children cannot be found in all Christendom," scientists based at Barrow, Alaska, with the 1882-1883 International Polar Expedition reported.

By imitating their parents' activities in play form, Eskimo children naturally and easily prepare themselves for their future role in life. Boys stalk snow buntings with small bows and arrows, girls mother dolls made of skins and carry them around in miniature *amautiks*. Many Eskimo games require considerable dexterity and some are of great antiquity, so old they are perhaps the common heritage of all mankind. One such game, at which the Eskimos excel, is cat's cradle. (This, incidentally, has nothing to do with cats. It is a corruption of "cratch cradle," an old word for the racks into which hay is put for cattle. In old English belief, the first figure of "cratch cradle" represented the manger cradle of the infant Christ.) With thong or sinew string, Eskimos could form a great variety of figures. Jenness, in a monograph on the string figures made by Copper Eskimos, lists more than a hundred variations. It is indicative of the wide distribution of this game that Jenness has also published a monograph on Papuan cat's cradles from New Guinea. One of the figures central and western Eskimos create shows the *kilifaiciaq*, the mammoth. Extinct for about ten thousand years, the memory of this Arctic elephant survives in this Eskimo game.

Equally ancient, perhaps, are some of the Eskimo folk tales. Though dressed in Eskimo garb, a few of these tales are strikingly similar to stories told in many other lands, bearing out, perhaps, Freud's statement about the universality of some folk tales which, he claimed, contain "the dreams of the human race."

Eskimos had no written language (the syllabic script now widely used in the central and eastern Arctic was introduced by missionaries), but legends and the memory of historical events were passed orally from generation to generation with great fidelity. Wilhelm Grimm, who with his brother Jacob collected the famous *Grimm's Fairy Tales*, noted already in 1815 the determined exactitude with which illiterate people transmit traditional tales. "Among people who follow the old ways of life without change, attachment to inherited patterns is stronger than we, impatient for variety, can realise."

Naturally, many Eskimo tales are coloured by sentiment. The Eskimos' ancient foes, the Indians, fare rather badly. *Itqilit*—"those with many louse eggs"—they are called and "old people have . . . told us that the Itqilit were half dog and half man, but we do not believe that their bodies were different from ours. We believe that their character as dog-men lies not in their bodies, but in their minds and manners," an Eskimo told Rasmussen. Greenland Eskimos, whose last contacts with Indians must have ceased at least 700 years ago, remember them in their legends and perpetuate a nearly subconscious dread of them. "Even as late as this, our twentieth century, the cry of 'Indians!' in an isolated southern Greenland settlement could throw the inhabitants into a state of senseless panic," Freuchen observed.

Greenland Eskimos also remembered another foe of former days: the Vikings who had settled on the west coast of Greenland before Thule culture Eskimos had reached Greenland. Eskimo legends have even preserved for five or six centuries the names of two Viking chieftains, Ungortok and Ulavik—Yngvar and Olaf.

Eskimos on Baffin Island call to this day "Kodlunarn" (White Man's Island) the small island near the entrance to Frobisher Bay where Martin Frobisher in 1577 found "good store of Ore, which in the washing helde golde plainly to be seene." He returned in 1578 with fifteen ships, mined two thousand tons of "gold ore" (fool's gold it turned out to be), and left the Eskimos of the region with a vivid oral tradition, quite accurate despite four centuries of retelling, of his travels and his work. When the American explorer Charles Francis Hall lived with Baffin Island Eskimos in 1861 an old woman told him "a great many years ago white men with great ships came. The first year [1576] one ship came [Frobisher's *Gabriel*], the second year three ships, and many ships the third year." When I visited Kodlunarn Island, a young Eskimo showed me a trench leading down to the sea and said: "This is where the white men repaired their ships." The contemporary chroniclers of the expedition, Settle and Best, do in fact record that ships were hauled up for repairs in just such a trench.

Tomassi Mangiok at Ivugivik, where Hudson Strait turns into Hudson Bay, one evening told me in great detail about the fight between Eskimos and Henry Hudson's mutinous crew at the murre colony on Digges Island in 1611. The tale was remarkably similar to, though seen from a somewhat different perspective from, the account written by one of the mutineers, Abacuk Prickket.

The white men, their habits, and their wealth were, of course, infinitely strange, fascinating, and occasionally frightening to Eskimos who saw them for the first time. Back and his crew, who descended the Great Fish River (now Back River) through the Barrens to the Arctic coast in 1833, were remembered, a century later, by the Uthuhikjalingmiut of Chantrey Inlet as "smiling men, who walked about with lumps of wood in their mouths emitting smoke." And Eskimos of the Pelly Bay area of the Gulf of Boothia remembered Sir John Ross and his companions quite vividly one hundred years after his expedition, but what left the most indelible impression was their ship. "However incredible it may sound, they [the white men] lived in a hollowed out floating island of wood that was full of iron and everything else that is precious in [our] land."

Slowly the old tales and traditions are being forgotten. In the settlements, the Eskimos' ancient hunting culture has all but ceased to exist and the long summer migrations of former days are only a memory of the older people. From the few camps left, Eskimos still travel far in summer in search of game, but overland migrations now are extremely rare. Kayaks have been replaced by motor-driven canoes, bow and arrow by guns, stone lamps and cooking pots by pressure stoves and metal utensils. But throughout the Arctic, from Alaska to Greenland, from the northernmost regions of Ellesmere Island to the remotest areas of the Barrens, one still finds the traces of the Eskimos' long migrations and travels of former days: collapsed stone caches; the lush vegetation covering ancient camp sites; the elaborate stone ambushes; the stone circles where men once had to await migrating caribou; the stone pillars, usually five or six feet high, where kayaks were laid up beyond reach of the forever hungry huskies; and, most frequently, the "tent rings," the row of stones that once held the lower edge of the Eskimo's tent in place. These remain, mute reminders of the people who travelled across this vast land, both barren and beautiful, during summers long since past.

O warmth of summer
    sweeping o'er the land!
Not a breath of wind,
Not a cloud,
And among the mountains
The grazing caribou.

Brightly coloured flowers bring colour to the Arctic during the short summer months.

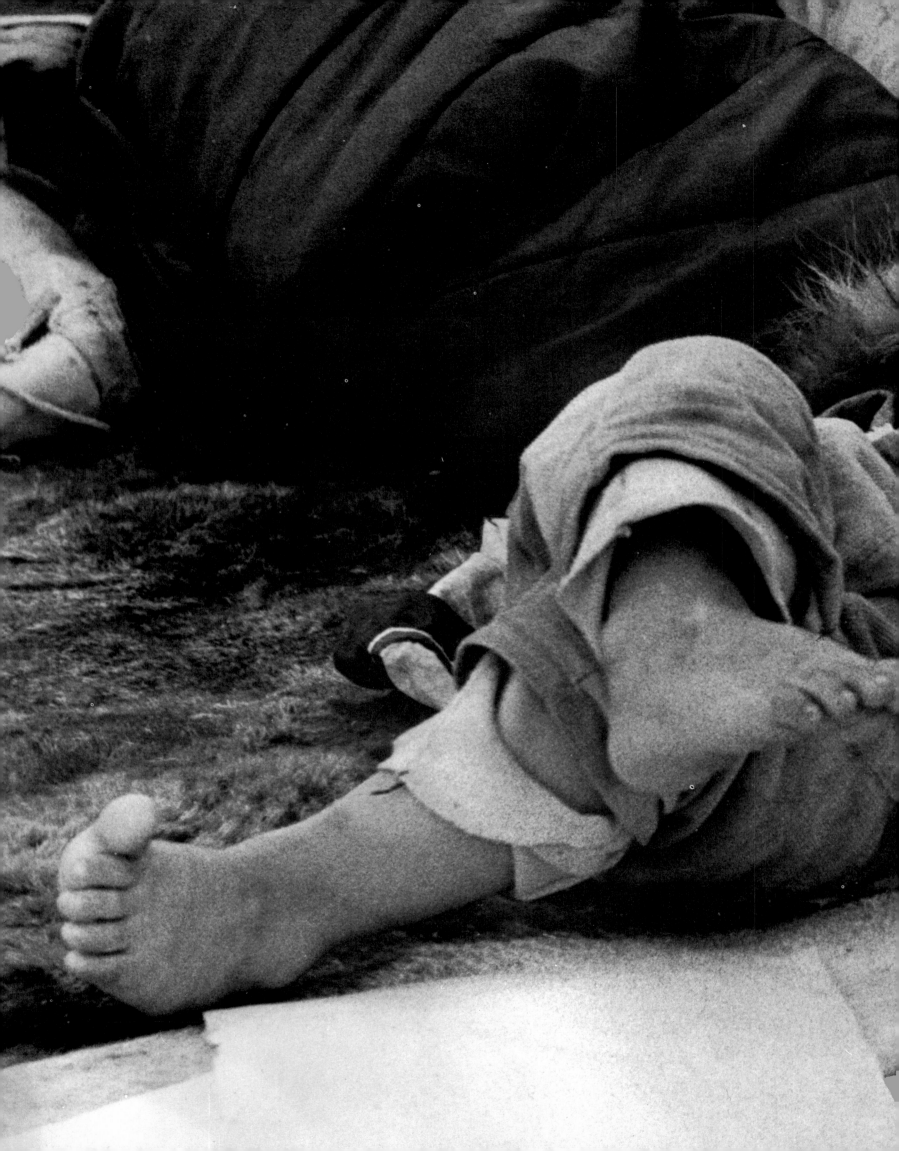

Below: An Eskimo makes faces to entertain his grandchild. Children are pampered and deeply loved. Eskimo philosophy holds that a child is innately good and, gently guided, will grow into a good adult. They are given great freedom, are rarely scolded, and never beaten.

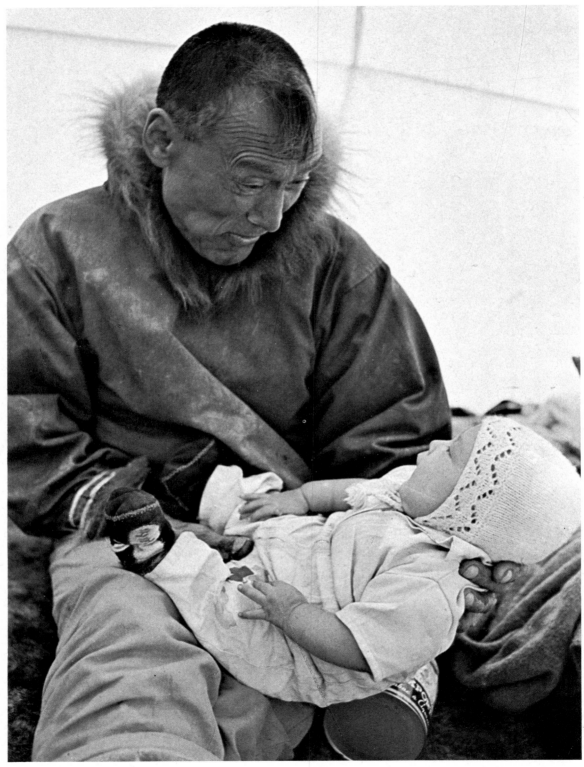

Right: Ammunition is expensive, and many camp Eskimos save money by pouring their own bullets. Bullet moulds they buy at northern stores. The lead they obtain by melting down shot, or the lead weights of old nets. Seal hunting in summer, in particular, requires a lot of ammunition, since the small bobbing head is a difficult target.

For the Eskimo woman, keeping her family well clothed is a nearly continuous job. The women in camp sew, cook, and take care of the children. The men hunt and fish, and make or repair their hunting and fishing gear. While his wife is busy sewing a new tent, an Eskimo readies his nets for char fishing in the fall.

Seals, in the past, were the basis of life for most Eskimos. Seal meat and blubber were their staple food. Seal oil warmed their homes. They used seal skins to make boots, pants, tents, and boats. Without seal, most of the Arctic would have been a land without people.

The endless search for food forces travel upon the Eskimo. Travel at breakup time is difficult. The ice is too weak for sledging, yet impedes boat travel. Shore leads provide a passage, but near capes hunters may have to pull their boat over the disintegrating ice.

An Eskimo holds a shot seal over the side of the canoe until it stops bleeding. Meat and blubber are either cached or taken back to camp.

fall

At Vostok, their scientific station on Antarctica, the Russians recorded in 1960 the lowest temperature ever measured on earth: −126.9° F. The Arctic, in comparison, is much milder, particularly the high Arctic coasts where temperatures rarely drop below −60°F., comparable to temperatures in some areas of Ontario, Manitoba, or even the northern United States. It is not the extreme cold, it is the extreme length of Arctic winter, nearly ten months in the high Arctic, that demands the utmost in endurance and adaptability from plants and animals.

If an Arctic summer is exceptionally cold, some "snow-bed" plants may not emerge at all from underneath deep drifts. But they survive, biding their time for another, more favourable year. Plant seeds, driven by wind onto ice, or into a rock desert, maintain the spark of life through decades of dormancy. Buried in permafrost, they can survive millennia. A lemming's cache of Arctic lupine seeds, hidden deep in the frozen ground more than ten thousand years ago, was recently discovered by botanists. Given earth and light and water, these seeds, asleep for one hundred centuries, awoke to life: they germinated, grew roots and flowers and new seeds. These delicate, lovely plants were older than mankind's recorded history.

In fall, Arctic life prepares itself for the rigours of the long winter ahead. The leaves of evergreen plants, such as Arctic white heather, lay in a rich store of starch, making them an important source of food to caribou and muskoxen wintering in the Arctic. Many plants develop next year's leaf and flower buds near or under the soil, and they store food in their root systems and rhizomes to be ready for next summer's growth. Arctic plants grow slowly, but they are exceptionally rich in sugars. Even the lowly lichens have a high carbohydrate content. Thus, although vegetation in the Arctic is often sparse, its nutritional value is relatively high, and in fall the herbivores are sleek and fat. Ground squirrels have nearly doubled their weight since they emerged from hibernation in spring. Their greatest enemy, the Barren Ground grizzly, swathed in a four-inch layer of fat, is ready for its long winter's sleep. Caribou, so emaciated in spring that sometimes even their marrow, the last reserve, is watery and fatless, now carry layers of back-fat, weighing as much as forty pounds, and their marrow is oily and rich.

The birds, too, accumulate stores of fat: those staying in the Arctic as insulation and energy reserve, the ones migrating south as a source of fuel. Ptarmigan snip off buds, bulbils, and leaves with single-minded concentration, as many as two to three thousand per hour until their crops grow large and distended. When winter comes, the ptarmigan are well protected by a thick layer of fat.

Tern chicks, only six or seven weeks old, are ready for their 11,000-mile flight. Golden plovers, their rumps neatly padded with a cushion of fat, fly from the eastern and central Arctic to Nova Scotia and New England, rest and restore their fat reserves, and then fly non-stop in forty-eight hours across the Western Atlantic to Guiana or Brazil, expending as much as one-third of their body weight in energy. The jaegers, gull-like birds with hawk-like habits, though quite capable of catching their own food, prefer to obtain it, where they can, by plundering that of terns and gulls. As the terns leave the Arctic so do the jaegers, and some continue to pester terns into giving up their food all the way down to Tierra del Fuego.

While all migratory birds fly south, away from the cold and darkness of Arctic winter, one bird heads north to the grim, floating ice desert of the Central Polar Basin. Ross's gull is among the smallest, least-known, and most beautiful members of the gull family, its plumage a delicate rose. It nests in Siberia, flies northeast in fall, passing the north tip of Alaska, and disappears northward in October into the Arctic night, surviving somehow, scientists assume, by finding food in leads among the shifting polar pack.

In late summer and fall, Arctic animals, in addition to laying up stores of fat, grow the thick winter fur or feathers that will enable them to withstand the cold and wind of winter. Caribou hairs are club-shaped, thicker at the tip than at the base, thus trapping air, a superb insulator, near the body. Each hair also contains numerous air cells, as added insulation. This air-filled fur is not only warm, it also makes the animals extremely buoyant, and caribou swimming across lakes or rivers float high in the water.

Muskoxen grow a thick layer of wool underneath their long cloak of guard hairs, which hangs nearly to the ground. This double-layered coat seems to render them impervious to the Arctic's worst cold and wind. Many Arctic animals change into winter white. Apart from camouflage, the white pelage or plumage serves as added protection against winter's searing cold. The pigment cells of the dark summer hairs are replaced by air cells in the white winter fur. Although a naked man begins to lose body heat at about 80° F., an Arctic fox, wrapped in dense, white, air-filled winter fur, loses heat only at temperatures 120 degrees lower than that.

The piebald plumage of the alcids of the north, auks, murres or puffins, and the penguins of the south, is their adaptation to cold. The white feathers on belly and breast, filled with air cells, form an insulating cushion against the sapping chill of the Arctic and Antarctic water on which they spend most of their lives. The dark back feathers, their cells filled with melanin granules, absorb the sun's warmth.

Encouraged by the warming trend of Arctic climate in recent decades, some "southern" animals are beginning to invade the Arctic. Moose wander far north in Labrador, deep into the zone formerly only occupied by caribou. In the central Arctic, moose reached Great Bear Lake in the 1880s, were seen near Coppermine in 1909, and now occur regularly in the Bathurst Inlet area of the Arctic mainland coast. Black bears have pushed north in recent years to Hudson Strait, invading the realm of the polar bear. Red foxes reached southern Baffin Island in 1918, were caught at the extreme north of Baffin Island in 1948, and by 1962 had reached Ellesmere, Canada's northernmost island. Seals have become rarer near parts of the now ice-free west Greenland coast, but they have been replaced by the economically more valuable Atlantic cod, moving northward in the warming water and now the basis of Greenland's most important industry.

It is generally believed that we are now in the waning period of the last Ice Age. During its peak, most of Canada and part of the United States (as well as Europe) was covered by mile-thick glaciers. So much water was locked within these ice sheets that the level of the world's oceans was three hundred feet lower than it is now, and two and a half million square miles (nearly equal to the land area of the United States) of now submerged continental shelf was exposed. Mammoths wandered far north across the now-vanished land of Beringia; vast deposits of mammoth bones and ivory are still found on the New Siberian Islands. But slowly the ice receded and the northern land, freed from the billion-ton burden (the glaciers were three miles thick in some areas), began to rise, as much as five inches per year at first, and in some regions six hundred feet and more in the last ten thousand years. Raised beaches mount terrace-like from the present coasts in many Arctic regions, and some of the oldest Eskimo camp sites, though once, no doubt, near the sea have since been raised to a remote inland level. In southern Baffin Island the post-glacial uplift has trapped Atlantic cod in a lake (called Ogac—Cod Lake—by Eskimos) so food-poor that these landlocked, giant-headed, spindly-bodied cod live mainly by eating each other. And high in the Ungava Peninsula, six hundred feet above sea level, harbour seals live in several lakes, locked in, too, perhaps by the rising land.

All the ice is not gone. Nearly three million cubic kilometers still press upon the Arctic land, and nine times that amount upon the Antarctic continent. Were this to melt, some areas of the Arctic would rise still higher, but much of the world, including most of its great cities would be below water as the land upon which they now stand once was, eons ago.

To all the vast upheavals of earth, nature has magnificently adapted over millions of years, forever changing, moulding, creating, spinning an interrelated and interdependent web of life for nearly every region of earth and sea. But the harsher the surroundings, the more delicate and tenuous the balance among plants and animals existing near the borderline of possible life. At few places on earth is this balance of nature more delicately poised than in the Arctic.

Long ago, the Eskimo lived in balance and harmony with nature. He was part of nature, subject to her laws a proficient predator, yet technically incapable of overexploiting the game resources or damaging the environment. The white man's first assault upon the Arctic was direct and drastic: he killed and, by supplying the Eskimo with superior weapons, enabled him to kill most Arctic wildlife. Whales were hunted to near oblivion; muskoxen were almost exterminated; of the 3,000,000 caribou of tundra and taiga, 200,000 were left; of the enormous walrus herds less than a tenth survived the slaughter; millions of seals were killed off Labrador. This wholesale destruction of Arctic animals deprived the Eskimos of the basis of their existence. To live, most depend now on work the white man provides or the humbling bounty of his welfare payments.

In theory, though, given proper protection, Arctic animals could have, in time, recouped their losses since the environment had not been damaged. Now a more insidious and potentially infinitely graver danger threatens the survival of all Arctic life: the destruction of the environment, the basis of its existence. Nature in the south, no matter how grievously polluted and disturbed, can heal herself if given the chance and time. In the Arctic, where growth is slow and decay even slower, damage done to the environment may turn out to be irremediable. While in warmer seas the more toxic parts of crude oil tend to evaporate first, the process of oil decomposition is very slow or stops entirely at freezing temperatures. One major oil spill in the far north could turn a large area of the Arctic into a biological desert.

Where tractor lugs rip up the thin plant cover that protects and insulates the Arctic soil, thermokarst sets in. The dark, exposed ground thaws deeply in summer, becomes unstable and subsides as much as three to four feet in a year. Subsequent thermal and water erosion can alter the topography of an entire region. A thermokarst trench, if sufficiently wide and deep, can impede caribou migration, keeping the animals away from vital grazing areas.

The fat of polar bears, even those killed in the high Arctic, has been found to contain considerable concentrations of DDT and DDT metabolite residues. The magnificent peregrine falcons, nearly extinct in eastern North America and increasingly rare in the west, are now also disappearing from the Arctic. Chlorinated hydrocarbons, derived through their food chain from DDT, cause them to lay thin-shelled eggs that do not hatch. As the falcons die out, falconers and collectors become more eager to possess them, paying as much as $6,000 for a peregrine and even more for the superb white gyrfalcons of the high Arctic, thus encouraging the raiding of their last eyries in the Arctic.

Since the first nuclear explosion in the world, Arctic lichen, which garner from the air natural fall-out particles, have begun to absorb more deadly substances: radioactive material filtering back to earth. Some of these lichens are the main food of caribou. Radioactive material, particularly Strontium-90 and Cesium-137, becomes concentrated in their bodies, often beyond the "safe" levels of man, and the milk of Eskimo mothers in Alaska who had eaten caribou meat was found to be radioactive contaminated.

Thus even in the isolation of their remote camps, the last Eskimos living on the land are affected, though unknowingly, by mankind's eternal preoccupation with war and destruction. When the anthropologist Diamond Jenness collected songs among Eskimos who had only recently come in contact with Europeans, he asked them to sing a war song. "They asked me what war meant," and when he explained (this was in 1915), the Eskimos were deeply disturbed and felt that "white men who deliberately used their extraordinary knowledge and powers for the wholesale massacre of each other were strangely unnatural and inhuman."

The Eskimos' struggle was not with other men (except for

occasional skirmishes with Indians) but for survival in a hard and implacable land. Fall for them, as for the animals and plants of the Arctic, was the season of preparation for the long, dark winter ahead. Fortunately for the Eskimos, fall is usually the north's season of plenty. The corpses of ringed seal sink when killed in summer, partly because their buoyant blubber layer is thin, partly because the influx of enormous quantities of fresh melt-water lowers the specific gravity of sea water. In fall, shot seals are fat and float and are easy to recover. Young seals, curious and inexperienced, are easily lured close to a boat by tapping a thwart or scraping the boat's bottom. The sounds, travelling far in water, fascinate the seals, who bob up closer and closer, until they are within gun range.

Char, who have spent two voracious months in the sea, now return fat to the lakes whence they came and where they will spawn later in fall. Char are powerful swimmers and have no trouble ascending rivers with strong rapids. But unlike their more southern relative, the salmon, they cannot hurtle themselves upward over even a small waterfall. The Eskimos took advantage of this, and barred the char's route with stone barriers and corrals called *sapotit*. As a large school of char swam into the sapotit, gaps in the stone traps were closed, men and women jumped into the icy water, and speared the fish with their long-handled, three-pronged leisters. Only the Eskimos of the far east and the far west knew and used nets to catch fish (and also seal); in the central Arctic the knowledge of nets had either died out or had never been developed. Here the Eskimos relied on stone weirs and spears. In a few areas until quite recently they also used ingenious traps made of plaited dwarf willow. Nearly identical fish traps are known from prehistoric middens in Denmark, dating back about eight thousand years, and they are also depicted in some of the earliest Egyptian tomb paintings.

Char, though slow-growing fish, are extremely numerous in many areas of the Arctic. Along the Labrador coast, north of Nain, Eskimos now net about 300,000 pounds annually. Near Wellington Bay, Victoria Island, Eskimos, operating a government-sponsored fishery and exploiting only one major river-lake system, catch 100,000 pounds of char a year on a sustained-yield basis.

The char caught by camp Eskimos are now, as in former days, split and air-dried on racks, long rows of blood-red fish so fat that on a warm fall day oil drips from them—energy-rich food for the winter.

Even more important than char are the caribou, for they supply the Eskimos with both food and clothing. Rasmussen once asked an Eskimo what he most desired of life. He answered: "I would like at all times to have the food I require, that is to say animals enough, and then the clothes that can shield me from wind and weather and cold. I would like to live without sadness and without pain, I mean without suffering of any kind, without sickness. And as a man I wish to be close to all kinds of animals so that in the hunt . . . I can excell over my countrymen. All that I desire for myself I desire also for those who through relationship are near to me in life."

To achieve freedom from want the hunters had to succeed in the fall caribou hunt. Forty caribou skins, short-haired and strong in fall, were required to dress a hunter and his family: eight skins for a man's complete winter suit, seven for a woman's, and four for a child's. Skins were needed to cover the sleeping platform, for sleeping robes, and to make caribou-skin tents. Cached dried char, caribou back-fat, and caribou meat were essential if the hunter and his family were to survive until seal hunting could begin in November or December. All Arctic land mammals accumulate fat reserves in fall and grow the thick fur that will protect them from cold. Ground squirrels cram their wintering burrow with food, and foxes in the high Arctic hide large caches of killed birds and lemmings. And the Eskimo, too, gets fur and fat for winter, and caches as many supplies as he can. Because early winter brings dearth and hardship.

In summer's continuous days everyone slept whenever he felt tired, be it day or be it night, since day and night were as one. Now darkness comes, each day a bit earlier, each morning a bit longer, until the sun is gone and it is always night. Auroras flare in the black sky, protons and electrons from the sun colliding with our atmosphere, white or greenish usually, but sometimes flaming in brilliant reds and greens, silent and superb. The Eskimos say they whisper in the winter night, and that if one whistles it will make them dance. The auroras are the souls of the dead, they once thought. "The souls of the good and those who commit suicide go to heaven where they play football with a walrus skull, which has life, and manifests its enjoyment of the game by chattering with its jaws. The Northern Lights are the spirits above at play," they told Franz Boas.

For one more instant, the north clothes itself in passionate colour, before adopting winter's stern dress of white and black: the flaming scarlet of bearberry leaves; the brick-red of creeping birches; the golden glow of willow; and, among the leaves, the rich reds and browns of sprouting mushrooms. Women and children spend days on end collecting berries: red, mealy bilberries; cloudberries, yellow when they are ripe, and amber-clear when frost has touched them; and the sourish, watery, black crowberries which Eskimos prefer above all others.

The mosquitoes are gone, and everyone moves outdoors. The men hunt whenever weather permits, or tend the char nets. They dig up peat to be used as shoeing on sled runners with mattocks made of curved pieces of antler. Sleds are repaired. New dog harnesses are made and old ones strengthened. As soon as caribou skins are dry, the women scrape them until they are as soft and smooth as chamois leather. In the past, Eskimos had many scrapers, each one serving a specific purpose: one to scrape seal skins; one curved, sharp and very strong for the initial scraping of caribou skins; one, scoop-shaped, to remove moisture from the sleeping platform. Once the scrapers were carved from bone or horn; now they are often a curious cultural hybrid, the handle still of horn, the blade made out of a tobacco or baking powder can.

More than we can ever imagine in our widely diversified society, with its infinite number of trades and crafts and industries providing the myriad things we need but are ourselves incapable of making (or consider ourselves incapable of making), the Eskimo in former days was self-sufficient and self-reliant. Whatever he needed, he made himself from the scant materials the Arctic provided. The Eskimos of the central Arctic mainland coast used native copper extensively, heating it first to fuse it, then hammering it cold into the desired shape with a stone or bone mallet. The Polar Eskimos used meteoric iron, found in the Cape York region of northwestern Greenland. But the main materials of all Eskimos were stone, bone, ivory, antler, driftwood, and in some areas baleen. From them they fashioned lamps and pots, drills and a multitude of ingenious weapons and traps, a considerable diversity of household utensils (such as spoons, ladles, back scratchers, scrapers, drinking tubes, drying racks, food dishes, containers, needles, and needle cases), sleds, boats, toys, and works of art.

Since an Eskimo had to make all the things that he and his family needed, he not only developed great manual dexterity, but also a frame of mind that made him look to himself for the solution of material problems. When the five hundred Eskimos of Povungnituk realized they could not possibly live by hunting any more and were encouraged to become "artists" instead, it probably never occurred to them to question their ability to make carvings and lithographs. They have a feeling of confidence that they can create, because they always had to rely solely upon themselves and their own skills to produce the things they needed. When Ekalun's automatic Swiss watch stopped, the old man's natural reaction was not to seek the help of a specialist, as southern man would have done, but to repair the watch himself. The tools he lacked, he made, and eventually he succeeded in repairing the watch.

Modern man is a small, specialized unit within a large, complex technological and cultural machine, which interrelates and intermeshes the abilities and skills of its constituent units, all contributing to the whole but none capable of existing on its own, and this sense of interdependence is deeply ingrained within our minds. The Eskimo was a complete unit all to himself, dependent upon no one. This fact shaped his mind and his attitudes, and made him both independent and self-assured in the subconscious knowledge that what he needed he could make. It is this spirit that enables an Eskimo to set out on a long trip with a minimum of food, weapons, and tools. If his spear shaft breaks, he will somehow make a new one. If a dog chews up a harness, the Eskimo somehow makes a workable substitute from an old pair of skin trousers. He is a master at improvisation, and when he is in trouble, he does not turn to others, he turns to himself and his own capabilities.

Considering the Eskimos' primitive tools of former days, one is amazed by the artifacts they managed to produce. Their secret was great manual skill, self-assurance, and infinite patience. Once, Rasmussen tells, in the land of the Netsilingmiut, a region nearly completely devoid of driftwood, "a mast drifted ashore, and of it they made sledges, kayaks and harpoons. The mast was split up by first making saws of barrel hoops; this took the whole of the summer and autumn, but time was not of much consequence if only they were able to utilize the valuable wood."

Most of the Eskimos' time was devoted to hunting, travelling, and making the tools, weapons, and clothes essential to their survival. But, as Franz Boas in his work on *Primitive Art* has pointed out: "No people known to us, however hard their lives may be, spend all their time, all their energies in the acquisition of food and shelter." Naturally, in making works of art, the Eskimos preferred those materials they habitually used in their work, just as people of the Magdalenian culture had done fifteen thousand years ago in Europe. Both peoples used similar materials and, as Jacquetta Hawkes in her book on the prehistory of man notes, "The working of bone, antler and ivory both for implements and works of art was brought to greater perfection by the Magdalenians than by any other primitive people. Their skill and artistry have been approached only by the Eskimos."

Much of early Eskimo art was decorative: utensils were embellished with engravings; utilitarian objects were gracefully carved in the shape of animals. Many of the small carvings were toys and games, whittled and polished with patience and skill during long, idle days of fall or winter, when weather made hunting impossible. And many of the early carvings must have been made, as similar carvings were made in Europe twenty thousand and more years ago, for religio-magical reasons, perhaps as amulets to promote success in hunting through sympathetic magic, perhaps to propitiate the spirits of killed animals, or maybe as spirit assistants to a shaman.

All things, the Eskimos once believed, had their "spirit' (though not necessarily a soul). The game of cat's cradle, for instance, had its own *inua;* it was possessed of a spirit, and care had to be taken not to offend it. If a hunter or his wife angered the string game's spirit, it might punish them. The man might harpoon a seal or walrus, and instead of running smoothly the line would entangle and drown him.

In most regions of the eastern Arctic, the Eskimos buried their dead under heaps of stones; sometimes they used huge slabs of stone to build quite elaborate tombs. In the central Arctic a corpse was wrapped in a caribou skin, and left on a ridge. In both areas, weapons and utensils were deposited with the dead, to be of use to them in afterlife. It was not the actual weapon that counted but its spirit. If a man needed a harpoon and knew of one left with a dead person, he could make a miniature replica and exchange it for the real harpoon, without depriving the dead of the essential "harpoon spirit." On a high ridge overlooking an old camp site at Bathurst Inlet, I once found scattered human bones. Near them was a box containing a full set of miniature weapons and, incongruously, a baking powder tin, containing small tools, fish hooks and lures. All these things had been left, so their spirits might accompany the dead man's soul.

Once Eskimos came in contact with whites, it did not take them long to discover that their ability to produce carvings was a marketable skill, and by and large in producing carvings for sale, they took their artistic cue from white man's tastes. Guided by the law of demand (and the fact that traders at one time bought stone carvings by weight!) their work changed from miniature to massive and, later, occasionally even to the monumental. Increasingly they used soapstone, although prehistoric steatite carvings are extremely rare.

Their work now varies from the extremely competent handicraft of a manually very skilful people, to impressive sculptures and lithographs made by truly inspired artists. Whatever its merit, it is not aboriginal art, as often claimed, since nothing like it was made by Eskimos in former days.

Eskimos probably never regarded carvings as an art, and even now most consider it as a salable skill; in fact few carvers are particularly fond of carving, most would prefer to hunt if they could make a living at it. Closer to art was the Eskimos' conception in former days of their songs and poetry and dancing. Songs, one said, "are thoughts, sung out with the breath when people are moved by great forces and ordinary speech no longer suffices." And they did love to sing. "There are so many occasions in one's life when a joy or a sorrow is felt in such a way that the desire comes to sing.... All my being is song, and I sing as I draw breath," an Eskimo told Rasmussen.

Often, Eskimos sang while they worked, to pass the time.

> Oft do I return
> To my little song.
> And patiently I hum it
> Above my fishing hole
> In the ice.
> This simple little song
> I can keep on humming
> I, who else too quickly
> Tire when fishing
> Up the stream.

Ekalun and his wife sang for hours, while he carved and she sewed clothes, entire tales, meandering through memory. At Rankin Inlet, where some twenty Eskimo artists work together in one large room, moulding ceramics, they nearly always sing when no white man is present, ballad-like songs of long ago.

Eskimo songs were generally of two kinds: ancient songs, some composed so long ago that their full meaning could not be clearly understood anymore and now belonging to an individual who had inherited them or to a group of people; and new songs, sometimes the result of considerable meditation, often extempore creations of an inspired singer at a song festival. In either case, they were strictly the private property of their creator, and only he was allowed to sing them.

In a special class were the lampoon songs. They were not easy to create since tradition demanded, in most areas, a fairly complex form. Typically a lampoon song started with a deceptively mild, tantalizing general introduction:

> Thinking of nobody in particular
> But people in general . . .

became more specific, and finally zeroed in on its victim with cutting mockery. Since everybody knew everybody else's business, the faintest allusion in the overture would already be understood and appreciated by the audience. Of course, not all Eskimos were gifted as poets and singers. Lamented one:

> A wonderful occupation
> Making songs!
> But all too often
> They are failures.

In song and poetry, Eskimos employed a wide variety of metaphoric substitute words, and singers who used many of these words, or invented new ones were widely admired. Thus *nanook* the polar bear became *pihoqahiaq*—the ever-wandering one; *oogpik* the arctic owl was *nangeqahijaq*—the always upright; *payneq* the caribou bull became *nagjuligjuaq*—the one with the big antlers, and *tarajoq* the sea (the word also means salt) is turned into *aquvijarjuaq*—the wide expanse where one hunts at the breathing holes.

In late fall, the people who during summer had scattered over the land began to cluster again into camps. Fishing and caribou hunting were finished, and the central Eskimos turned their backs to the land and looked again to the sea and its seals to provide them with food. For the women, sewing winter clothes, it was a busy period. For the men, it was a rare season of relative idleness.

As darkness descended upon the north, many Eskimos were gripped by a feeling of doom and dread. "Hysteria is peculiarly common around the Polar basin; the long winter darkness and the loneliness and silence of the hunter's life make the Arctic peoples more susceptible to this disorder than the rest of the human race," Diamond Jenness noted. And among the Netsilingmiut, Rasmussen "observed the same thing as so often before at Thule in North Greenland, that the approaching darkness and the long stormy nights affected the nerves and minds of the Eskimos . . . . Anxiety was in their blood and the spirits continued to haunt them."

> There is fear
> In feeling cold
> Come to the great world
> And seeing the moon
> —Now new moon, now full moon—
> Follow its old footprints
> In the winter night.

Yet the worst famine the Netsilik Eskimos can remember in the hunger-haunted oral history of their people occurred more than a century ago, during "the year when winter did not come." The caribou migrated south, and so did the birds. But it remained mild, and the Netsilingmiut, who did not use kayaks for sea hunting, sat in their tents near the shore, waiting for ice to form so they could hunt seal at their breathing holes.

But the sea did not freeze; the people starved, and the survivors ate the dead. "Hunger holds terrors; hunger is always accompanied by dreams and visions that may destroy even the strongest man and make him do things he would otherwise detest. So we never condemn those who have eaten human flesh; we have only pity for them.... In particular, we take strict care that such people never eat the meat of bears or ravens. That meat is like human meat, and we fear that the memory of their misery will drive them mad."

Late fall and early winter were the Eskimos' most festive season, partly because they had time to spare, partly, perhaps, to counteract a certain subconscious dread of winter and darkness. It was a time for games and story telling, for song and dancing, all probably essential during this dark and dreary period of the year to avoid that boredom which, as the Danish philosopher Sören Kierkegaard has pointed out, leads to "emotional starvation."

Their chief distractions were song festivals and drum dances. The Eskimo drum, really a large tambour, was held with one hand by a handle attached to its rim. The dancer turned the drum on its axis, beating its wooden rim with a short, stout drumstick. It was a nearly stationary dance, most of the movement being in the knees, the body swaying back and forth.

Once the ice was strong and covered by snow, deep and hard enough to build igloos, the people of the central Arctic left the land and built their winter villages far out on the sea ice. The agloo hunting of winter commenced, and their lives moved on in harmony with and dependent upon the eternal cycle of the seasons.

Eskimos in the past conceived of all nature as a spiritual unit of which they were a part. Inanimate objects had their spirits, just as animals and men had their souls. An Eskimo who had never before met white men told Rasmussen: "The only thing of value in a man is his soul. That is why it is the soul that is given everlasting life....When a man dies, the soul leaves the body and the body remains on earth and rots, whereas the soul goes on living." Killed animals had to be treated with the greatest respect, and an Igloolik Eskimo has pointed out that, "Life's greatest danger lies in the fact that man's food consists entirely of souls." To propitiate the souls of the dead, animal as well as human, Eskimos observed a vast array of taboos, and their shamans did their best to prod or placate those that ruled all life.

In the collision of cultures when white men began to invade the Arctic, that of the Eskimos, inevitably, suffered. "To kill a culture," the ethologist Konrad Lorenz observes in his book *On Aggression,* "it is often sufficient to bring it into contact with another, particularly if the latter is higher, or is at least regarded as higher." Although Eskimos instantly acknowledged the white man's technological supremacy, they were not so quick to admit his superiority in other fields. A Netsilik Eskimo told Rasmussen: "It is generally believed that white men have quite the same minds as small children. Therefore one should always give way to them. They are easily angered, and when they cannot get their will they are moody and, like children, have the strangest ideas and fancies."

Once they were brought into settlements, the old continuity of Eskimo life ceased. No longer was "the past of the adults . . . the future of each new generation," as the anthropologist Margaret Mead has put it. The children were educated in white man's schools in white man's language for the white man's way of life, learning about "Dick and Jane on the farm," and subjects similarly remote from their ancestral way of life and, only too often, without relevance to even today's life in the north.

In some areas even the Eskimo language is dying out. In Hopedale, Labrador, some grandparents who speak only Eskimo now need interpreters to communicate with their grandchildren who speak only English.

If their former life was physically harder, it was emotionally more secure than the Eskimos' present existence between a dead past and an uncertain future. "The pre-European Eskimos," Diamond Jenness has said, "were healthy . . . cheerful and relatively contented—far more contented, I believe, than their present-day descendants, or their white fellow countrymen whose restless civilization, with its mélange of virtues and vices, they are slowly learning to assimilate."

The days of the self-reliant Eskimo hunter, living off the land, are nearly over. Only in a few camps are old traditions and lore preserved; families still mould their lives to the ancient rhythm of the seasons; and at least part of the Eskimos' ancient culture, attuned to their harsh land, persists. Theirs is a vanishing way of life. It was a hard life, but it possessed the harmony and balance that comes when men are free within themselves, secure within their society, and imbued with a feeling of kinship with all nature.

Glorious was life
Now I am filled with joy
For every time a dawn
Makes white the sky of night
For every time the sun goes up
Over the heavens.

There is fear
In feeling cold
Come to the great world
And seeing the moon
– Now new moon, now full moon –
Follow its old footprints.

Split char hang on the Eskimos' drying racks in fall — energy-rich food for the winter months. Caches of dried fish and dried caribou meat tide the Eskimos over the lean days of early winter, until the ice is strong enough to permit seal hunting. After the men return from fishing, the women and children split and gut the day's catch of whitefish and char.

Below: A fishing camp at a lonely Arctic cove.

Right: Walrus bones litter a beach on tiny Bencas Island in Hudson Bay, where long ago Eskimos cut up their kills.

Left: In camp, looking after the children is woman's work. But during the migrations, father is expected to do his share. Eskimos now swaddle babies in cloth diapers; in former days they used fur diapers or absorbent moss. Children are "toilet trained" as early as possible.

Right: A fur-clad father washes his child, despite the cold in the tent. Eskimo children in camps are healthy and hardy, and their parents think nothing of changing children's clothes or washing a baby at sub-zero temperatures.

Above: A chess set, carved by Ekalun of Bathurst Inlet: the rooks are igloos; the bishops, dogs; the knights, polar bears rampant; the king and queen, Eskimos in full fur regalia; and the pawns, obese little Arctic owls. Chess figures and board squares are carved from different-coloured soapstone.

Left: Carving has always been an essential Eskimo skill. Of bone, stone, ivory, or horn, they carved toggles for dog harnesses, spoons, cooking pots, harpoons, fish spears, or sled parts. Now, when bad weather permits, camp Eskimos carve works of art for the white man's market.

Left: Tents and boats of an Eskimo camp, mirrored in Bathurst Inlet.

Above: Caribou migrate southward across the vastness of Canada's Barren Grounds.

Left: Caribou shot near the coast are dragged to shore and brought by boat to camp.

Above: Two stones, a caribou liver spit on the tine of caribou antler, a low fire of Arctic heather: these make up a tundra feast after a long day's hunt.

Left: With her ulu, the crescent-shaped woman's knife, the wife of a hunter cuts caribou meat into thin slabs, so it can be dried and stored. Leg bones are cleaned and set aside for a feast; raw or boiled marrow is one of the Eskimos' favourite delicacies.

Right: An Eskimo admires the magnificently curved caribou antlers that an ancestor of his left long ago on an Arctic beach. Bleached by sun and wind and water, the antlers may be a decade old—or a century. Decay in the Arctic is extremely slow.

After a successful hunt, an Eskimo carries the quartered caribou back to camp in a large canvas satchel. Eskimos carry heavy loads with a tumpline and lines across the upper arms and chest, and thus walk tirelessly for hours.

Above: Caribou-skin tents have nearly dried out. Only a few Eskimos still use them. They are much warmer than canvas tents, but dark—despite the seal-gut window near the gable—and bulky and, if they get waterlogged, extremely heavy. Dry tents, on the other hand, are so buoyant that Eskimos in the past used them as rafts to cross rivers during their migrations.

Left: A family travels overland in search of caribou. In the past, Eskimos migrated thus for months, carrying everything they needed with them. Each pack-dog carries, in sausage-shaped bags, supplies weighing forty or fifty pounds. But many dogs don't like it and try to shed their load, preferably while crossing a creek.

Fall brings vivid colours to the tundra: the glow of red bearberry leaves and the golden yellow of dwarf willow. With the first frost, mosquitoes vanish; hares and foxes change into winter camouflage, and soon the snow will change the north again into a land of black and white.

Berries grow in rich profusion in the valleys and on the hillsides of the north. Women and children collect them in fall, but all are eaten and none are stored for winter. For the Eskimos this is the Arctic's time of plenty: fat char ascend the rivers; caribou are fat and their fur suitable for winter clothing; and sleek seals float when killed and are easily retrieved.